TIME WAS MINE

Time was Mine is Derek Tangye's account of his journey round the world as a young man. Recalling his voyage via America, the South Sea Islands, Australia, New Zealand, Japan, China, Russia (on the Trans-Siberian railway) and Germany—tasting romance in Tahiti and glimpsing thirties Hollywood—he makes discerning observations of a world about to be transformed by war and captures all the excitement of youthful adventure.

GW00775944

TIME WAS MINE

Derek Tangye

CHIVERS LARGE PRINT
BATH

British Library Cataloguing in Publication Data available

This Large Print edition published by Chivers Press, Bath, 1995.

Published by arrangement with Michael Joseph Limited.

U.K. Hardcover ISBN 0 7451 3157 3
U.K. Softcover   ISBN 0 7451 3165 4

Photoset, printed and bound in Great Britain by
Redwood Books, Trowbridge, Wiltshire

TIME WAS MINE

Time Was Mine was the reason why I met Jeannie. Had it not been for *Time Was Mine*, I would not have written *A Gull on the Roof*, *A Cat at the Window* or any of the other Minack Chronicles. Nor would Jeannie have written *Meet Me at the Savoy*, or her trilogy of hotel novels, *Hotel Regina, Home is the Hotel* and *Bertioni's Hotel*.

I was in the front hall of the Savoy Hotel soon after *Time Was Mine* was published. It was the period when bombs were falling on London. I was standing there when a friend said, 'See that very pretty girl over there? She is Jean Nicol, and she is in charge of Savoy publicity. You must meet her. She could arrange to have *Time Was Mine* placed prominently on the bookstall.'

Thus I met Jeannie.

'Will you put my book on the bookstall?' I rushed out.

And she did.

A week later I saw her again.

'I loved your book,' she said.

I was relieved.

Time Was Mine, telling of my journey round the world, had been condemned by the vicar

1

from the pulpit of my family's local church, much to the amusement of my father and mother to whom I dedicated the book, and both of whom were in the congregation; and shortly after we were married and were living at Mortlake overlooking the Thames, a neighbour said to another neighbour, 'I *do* hope Mrs Tangye hasn't read Mr Tangye's book'.

But Jeannie had read the book and told me she loved it.

'Well,' I had replied, 'will you have dinner with me?'

The Minack Chronicles story had begun.

CHAPTER ONE

GOODBYE TO THE BEGINNING

Thirty minutes to go. I had a hollow feeling inside, reminding me of tearful partings ending happy holidays. I needed a drink. My father had disappeared to buy the platform tickets so it was Mother who accompanied me to the bar. I remember she had a light sherry and I, not wanting her to hear my order, asked the red-haired barmaid in a whisper for a double brandy. I drank it as I would water, and the effect was delightful. I walked off to the platform with a hazy confidence that made chatter easy; what a pity that in the old days of the school train I couldn't go to the bar, in place of stuffing myself with cream buns in a farewell tea.

Fifteen minutes to go. The platform bustled with Americans searching for their seats, and porters wheeling cabin trunks plastered with coloured labels. My father had found my compartment and was standing by the door with Janet Johnson; Jan provokingly attractive in a black velvet coat with cuffs and collar edged with white ermine, and a single gardenia in her black hair. And there too were Clifford Evans, Clement Fuller and Brian Chapman; laughing they were as if a bride and bridegroom off on their honeymoon were the cause of their presence, not me by myself. Then Nigel, my brother, and Ann Todd arrived; Ann with a small Cossack hat perched on her head, and looking so lovely that the group in the next compartment halted their goodbyes to stare.

Five minutes to go. Colin, my eldest brother, came hurrying up the platform. We talked of 'remembering to write.' Then Mother mentioned my keys. She wanted me to have two sets each with a key of my two suitcases. So as we talked, she tied with string my four keys into two bunches. 'You can lose one set now, dear,' she said, 'because you'll have the other.' But that evening in my cabin I discovered she had tied the same two keys on each bunch.

Two minutes to go. Porters were shouting: 'Take your seats, please!' I shook hands. Someone said: 'I wonder what will have happened...' Then Nigel making us all laugh, asked: 'A little domestic matter ... what is it I pay Mrs Moon each week?' I kissed Mother. Colin pushed three £1 notes into my hand. My father said: 'Give my love to the South Sea maidens.' The whistle blew.

I couldn't see them for long. There's a curve on that Waterloo platform. My father was the last one, standing alone waving his black Homburg hat. Then he too was gone. The train gathered speed, past the blocks of grey warehouses, past the backyards of the soot-covered Vauxhall slums. Faster, faster. I

4

chucked the stub of my cigarette on the track, watching the sparks for a second dance between the sleepers before we left them behind. Then I pulled up the window and sat down. The journey had begun.

2

It had begun in my mind nine years before, when, aged seventeen, I was wondering what to do with my life while others were wondering what to do with me. My Harrow schooling wasn't meeting with the success that warranted its expense. Term reports were littered with 'Could do better if he tried'—'Doesn't seem to concentrate,' and my housemaster would bi-weekly tell me I wasn't pulling my weight in the house.

The criticisms were largely justifiable. For my part I could find no sense in learning ten verses of the Bible every Sunday evening; nor in translating Latin Unseen when my interest lay in modern languages; nor in being examined about a Shakespeare play as if it were a grammar book. The masters, in my youthful opinion, were fools to bother about such things. They bothered, of course, because the line dividing the brain from a dunce in a public school is the Oxford and Cambridge Certificate. In fact, on the second occasion I failed in this test my housemaster described me as being 'Simply useless to society, old man.'

It was amid this depressing state of affairs

that the family and I debated my future. It was my own ambition to become a writer, not for any love of words, but because I believed a writer had a more exciting time than most people; and it was with this in view that I had secretly paid £7 for a course in journalism— which I studied underneath the bedclothes of my school-bed aided by a torch when lights were out. Neither I nor the Principal thought much of the results; and on reaching the fifth lesson he advised me to concentrate on my school examinations and leave journalism to a later day. Then it was that the idea was born of making my way round the world. What I needed, I thought, was experience, and a year in the world ought to provide me with enough of it to start me on the road to journalistic success. It was, of course, an old idea; and like the thousands of young men who had had the same idea before me, it didn't materialize. Such an adventure cannot be made on air; and money wasn't plentiful. Besides, despite my protests of 'You don't understand!' my family didn't think me responsible enough to be let loose in the world. The idea had to be shelved, but it was not forgotten; there would come a time, I felt certain, when my ambition would be realized.

Thus on leaving Harrow I became an office boy in one of those mammoth organizations whose employees are nursed by a staff manager and a corps of assistants. In my case, the staff manager was a fat man with pince-nez who waggled a finger at me and assured me that I had only to show zest in my work to be promoted to a traineeship, a managership in embryo. The first six months therefore witnessed a ferocious enthusiasm on my part. I read books on economics. I studied the *Financial Times*. I arrived thirty minutes before the others in my department so as to sort out the morning mail. I worked overtime in the evening. I enrolled in a commercial course at a correspondence school. And at the end of this period my salary was raised 1*s. 3d.* The rise coincided with a damping of zeal. Bills of Lading began to lose their glamour. Standing in the eight-thirty with the same blank faces no longer amusing. Running errands a bore. And, besides, two things had happened.

The first was my entrance into débutante society. The old Harrovian tie was a magic wand that brought me dumb girls and champagne hangovers. Five days a week I would clamber into bed at dawn and four hours later wish the world would end. Through the day the wish remained—until I hurried from the office to the cocktail party where I was likely to find the strongest sidecars.

The second was a book I'd read called *Through Literature to Life*, by Ernest Raymond. This somewhat balanced my youthful exuberance among the débutantes. It was a book that if I had been given to read

7

when I was fourteen would have stopped me wasting my time at school. Ernest Raymond said in it what my schoolmasters didn't say. He told me what to read from the point of view of pleasure, of enrichment of the mind. He transformed Shakespeare, the Bible, Shelley, Byron, from the category of dreary lesson subjects into books of wisdom and beauty. I heard for the first time of Flaubert, de Keyserling, and Proust. He awoke in me an awareness of the beat of life. I wished only that I had read before these words of his on education:

'There is only one stable theory of education. It is this; that if I were a headmaster and had to choose my assistants, whether they were to teach mathematics or Latin, chemistry or cricket, I would favour those who had a fine proselytizing enthusiasm for literature and art, even though their manners were atrocious and their methods abominable; because it is chiefly in the things of art that the fire of imagination is lit; and hence the master will possess imagination, penetration and sympathy, and he will light up in his pupils their smouldering humour, their essential humanity, their inalienable hunger for beauty, and their inborn desire to create beauty for themselves; which things it is the final business of education to educe.'

Both Ernest Raymond and the débutantes had a bad effect on my business career. Both bared the dreariness of sitting at an office desk however important one might become. The one making plain that women and rigid office hours didn't mix; the other firing me with the excitement of living. Once again I decided journalism should be my career; and in my spare time I wrote articles on a variety of subjects which editors regularly returned. This didn't dishearten me because I never really expected to have one published. I had such an inferiority complex that I looked at a journalist with the same scared eyes as an office boy looks at the chairman of the company. So when the miracle occurred and five hundred words on the subject of an archery competition was published in the *News Chronicle*, I felt like the dustman who won the first prize in the Irish Sweep.

That same week I visited a phrenologist who murmured three times, 'You must not barter!' and who went on to say that my bumps displayed a preference for advertising and literary work. So when the day afterwards I was told by the fat man with pince-nez that I had been promoted to selling soap from house to house in Wigan, I sensed fate had warned me to do otherwise and I refused his offer. Moreover, a few days later I sent in my notice, and the fact that I did so was because I have a very exceptional father and mother. It was their belief that a young man shouldn't have to grind along in a career in which he had no interest. Better be in a job one enjoyed than a success in a job one hated. With no prospects on the horizon they let me give up a steady pay packet in return for an allowance of £2 a week and gamble that I would find a place in the career I wanted.

The next five months were uneventful. I wrote more articles which rebounded with regularity. Débutante parties continued. A job seemed as far off as ever. My principal occupation was operating a race-horse system in which Mother and I believed lay a fortune. It involved betting varying sums on six horses a day. The time required each morning to discover which were the horses varied between two and three hours; and the afternoons were spent standing at street corners waiting for the latest editions. The partnership was not successful. At the end of three months we were lucky to find our capital was as we began; and we decided to call it a day.

In the sixth month I had an interview with Max Aitken and from it was given a month's trial on the *Daily Express* in Manchester. The suddenness of the opportunity startled me. The most I'd expected from the interview was an introduction to a provincial editor, so when I found myself at a typewriter in the reporters' room of a national daily I felt like a fourth-form boy sitting among his prefects. Office days being still fresh in my memory, I was also ready for friction with my fellow-workers; I expected them to cold-shoulder me because of my inexperience; I imagined that they would enjoy showing their superiority over a newcomer; and, in fact, that the month would be one of the most unpleasant besides being one of the most important of my life. Of course I was wrong. From the moment I met Brian Chapman, the editor, who, in place of an orthodox interview, told me a funny story about a Liverpool civic dignitary whose head went through the roof of an aeroplane in a storm, I knew it was going to be all right. Further proof came when next day on the first story I was ever sent out to cover, the reporter who was my guide took me to the local pub for an hour before he showed any interest in the news we'd been told to collect. So when the month was over and Brian Chapman took me on the staff, there was no one so happy that day as I.

The work was as exciting as I expected. I interviewed politicians, bishops, and actresses. I hunted the city at night for burglars and outbreaks of fires. I questioned mothers of lost daughters and husbands of lost wives. Many of the things I did were not pleasant; yet such was the fever of news-gathering that all my sense of decency was smothered and I was unconscious of my callousness. There was the evening I was sent off to interview an old couple whose son, a missionary, was believed to have been murdered by Chinese bandits. Taking a leaf from the book of a confidence trickster I talked on every kind of subject before I disclosed I was a newspaper reporter; and by that time I was sitting in their kitchen having a cup of tea. Having come so far I racked my brains for a novel angle to my story. Suddenly I had a bright idea. We should kneel down and pray for the son's safety. The old man brought out his Bible and the three of us knelt in prayer— simply because I had seen in my mind the morrow's headlines describing the event. Another evening sticks in my memory. Cold rain was driving through the cobbled streets of Blackburn. The mill girls, shawls round their heads, were hurrying home to their grey-stoned cottages. I buttoned the collar of my raincoat as I got out of the car to knock at the door of one. A woman opened it; her face was lined, her skin yellowish, and I noticed the puffs under her eyes before I noticed the eyes themselves; to a stranger in the north she looked middle-aged, but I do not think she was more than thirty. Behind her were four ragamuffin children who were standing shyly watching the strange man at the door. I did not know how to begin. This was the first time that I had broken the news of death. Yet it was my job to tell this woman that her husband, a lorry driver, had been killed in an accident. I took her into a room away from the children. I remember how I expected her immediate reaction would be a flood of tears and how I was surprised at the calm way she behaved. It emboldened me to ask her for a picture of her husband and she took one from where it was standing on the mantelpiece. As she handed it to me, her control snapped and she collapsed sobbing on the floor. I left her there and ran out to get the help of a neighbour. But as I did so I remember I was thinking not of the woman, but of the story I had, and the picture I held in my hand.

4

London on a Sunday newspaper followed Manchester. Then a year in the film industry and back again on a Sunday newspaper. I was writing articles for magazines as well, some of which were accepted; a particular one was read by an editor of the *Daily Mirror* who was looking for a columnist. The subject dealt with my likes and dislikes and pleased the editor in question: at any rate, he sent for me, invited me to join his staff and offered a salary twice as much as I'd hoped for. The consequences were remarkable. I was transformed overnight from a hack journalist who was lucky to see his name in print into a 'celebrity' whose articles each morning were headlined: 'This brilliant young writer'—'He writes another stirring article today'—'Derek Tangye Denounces

Hypocrisy', etc. It was highly amusing, and the more extravagant the praises, the more the family and I laughed. When in addition my photograph came careering down the streets of London on the tops of buses, my father gave a celebration party. No fame so strange nor so sudden had ever come to the family before.

That was the humorous side. The serious side was that the kind of column I wrote, laughed at by the intelligentsia for its admitted lack of virility, was in fact an important influence in many people's lives. Godfrey Winn, of course, began the style. He dotted his page with homely truths and the Christian names of stage figures, peers, and peeresses until he became a sort of Sir Galahad and Father Confessor in one; to his readers he appeared to have the glamour of a film star and the patience of a parson; at any rate, five hundred of them used to write to him every day. All those letters he answered personally, besides seeing a score or so of his readers every afternoon in his office; it meant that in a single week he did more practical good than most journalists do in a lifetime. For my part I was amazed at the power that was mine. There was a fund, for instance, from which I drew money to help hard-luck stories that I believed to be genuine; the fund was solely supported by the generosity of readers, and whenever it became low, I had only to appeal in my page, and the postal orders would come rolling in. Then

14

there were the secrets I was expected to share and the advice to give. A girl came to me one morning with the confession she had been stealing from the petty-cash desk of her shop. What was she to do? Another, that she had run away from home because she was going to have a baby. There was the young man whose girl wife had been taken to a lunatic asylum and he wanted to know what future there was for his two-year-old child. There was the middle-aged woman who could not make up her mind whether to tell her husband that the doctor had warned her she had only twelve months to live. There were scores of cases like these, and it was my privilege to try to unravel their problems or at least show my sympathy. But many a time, when I sat in my chair listening to the outpourings of some unfortunate person, I thought how silly it was that I should be the counsellor. After all, I only held the position because of the whim of an editor; one word from him and down from the pedestal I'd fall.

Eventually the word came; and as it is the reason why I'm writing this book I'll tell you what happened. One fine morning my chief called me into his office and informed me that he was most satisfied with my work and wished to lengthen my contract. A few days later it was further decided that I should visit, each weekend at the newspaper's expense, the capitals of Europe, starting off with Paris the coming weekend. That was on a Thursday. On

15

Friday I had come into the office, with my suitcase and my seat booked on the afternoon plane, when my chief had another idea. I was politely informed that he had changed his mind, the policy of the paper had been altered overnight, and my column wasn't wanted any more.

The news, to say the least, was a shock. The ways of Fleet Street are always unexpected, but even so I wasn't prepared for anything quite so abrupt. The blow, however, was immediately softened by the presentation of a large sum of money—produced in the spirit of generosity towards discarded employees that only Fleet Street knows. It eased the situation, but it didn't remove me from the tight corner I found myself facing. I walked out of the office in a daze, and made my way to the Falstaff, where I ordered a large brandy.

While I sipped it I wondered what I should do. I had to act fast, as I was more likely to land a good job before the news leaked out than afterwards. On the other hand, where was there a vacancy for my type of column? Jobs like mine were few and far between. I didn't relish the thought of being pointed out as the young man who skyrocketed to fame, and then fell back to where he began; and yet, if this should happen, it would not be without justification. I was typical of other young men whose success was a pretence, achieved by luck, and not as the result of experience. The

16

kind whose monetary rewards have tempted them to believe so much in their own importance that they have basked in their success until their spirit of adventure had been numbed, and they have been tied hand and foot to the routine of their comfortable lives. I knew that I would become the same as these; that, supposing my chief hadn't fired me, I would have gone on writing my column and handing out advice, until my own spirit was undermined and I fizzled out like a damp squib.

As I was thinking this, it dawned on me that never before had I possessed enough capital to finance a long journey abroad, and that it was nine years since first I had the idea of going round the world. In that time I'd known both failure and a measure of success, and I'd learnt that, though I enjoyed the pleasures that money could bring, I could in certain circumstances be just as happy as if I were broke. I'd realized, too, that ever since my schooldays my chief ambition had been to live vividly—not to be afraid of making mistakes, only afraid of having to regret things I hadn't the courage to do; and if by doing so I made a fool of myself, I was prepared to take heed of the fact. I wanted to achieve peace of mind, but how, I hadn't discovered, though I believed that this might be done, if, when I was old, I could look back on the years and say: 'I have lived.' The world was there for me to see. I was a good deal more fitted to journey into it than when I was a schoolboy. I was now a moderate craftsman in a profession which it was possible to practise wherever pen and paper were to hand. I was without a job and had no ties; and therefore had nothing to lose by going. I had money, but not much; the lack of it would give added spice to the journey, and make it necessary for me to use my wits. And whatever happened, when it was all over, I would still have my memories. 'I'll go,' I said to myself, and paying for my drink I went up the stairs to the street.

*   *   *

That, therefore, was how it came about that I was sitting in the Southampton boat train as it tore through the green fields of Surrey and Hampshire towards the *Aquitania* and New York.

I had told my chief my plan, and with his blessing I had written an article on what I was going to do. I said I was going away for a year to see the world. I wasn't going to take the journey too seriously, my main object being to enjoy myself; so that if I made mistakes or any illusions were broken I would try to see the funny side. I said I was going to wander as I pleased. If I liked a place I might stay a month; if I didn't, I'd move on. I had no fixed plans. Time was mine to do what I liked with.

CHAPTER TWO

NEW YORK SAYS 'NUTS'!

Four hundred and fifty pounds was what I had for my travels. Of this sum, £50 had already been spent on the fare to America and a £100 in Traveller's Cheques was tucked in my wallet. The balance I had entrusted to my father who was to forward me parts of it in answer to each SOS. The sum seemed scarcely enough to pay for a year's travelling, but my intentions were to earn more by writing; for this purpose New York seemed a good starting-point.

Like most people, I nursed certain ideas about New York. I pictured it as the most go-ahead and most hospitable city in the world—and more so than any other city in America. So many of my friends and acquaintances had returned from it, glorifying the generosity and initiative of its citizens above those of their own country, that I was sure I merely had to blow my trumpet loud enough for the contracts and invitations to come rolling in. In this belief I was encouraged by, among others, a publicity friend of mine who insisted on sending ahead of me, to editors of newspapers and magazines, a remarkable pamphlet describing my career in the language of a film producer announcing a new star. Not content with that, he was to gild the lily by cabling the day before my arrival: 'Watch out for Derek Tangye *Aquitania* tomorrow.' He seemed certain that the editors, as a result, would be scrambling over each other in competition to hire me as a guest columnist; that hotels would offer me free rooms, restaurants free meals, and theatres free seats. I would, in fact, 'put one over' on New York.

It was in this mood of expectation that I awoke in my state-room one Tuesday morning as the *Aquitania* neared New York. The state-room, so I'd been told, was as essential to me as books to a library. Americans measured success by the money spent, and if an influential passenger or a reporter discovered I had a poky little inside cabin, they would have nothing further to do with me. I therefore spent in five days what normally would have lasted five weeks.

Unhappily there were no influential passengers. The decks were as bare of celebrities as Brighton pier on a winter's night. I was not unduly upset; because, after all, the reporters were the more important; and I'd planned that as soon as they'd asked for me, I'd invite them to the state-room and load them with drinks as if I were a millionaire.

First, however, I wanted to see the skyline I'd heard so much about. We were due to dock at ten, so I was up at seven, dressed in a summer suit in anticipation of the sunshine a New

20

Yorker, the night before, had warned me would greet our arrival. Up on deck I went, fieldglasses in hand (and even a notebook to record my impressions), only to get as big a surprise as if I'd found snow on a tropical island. No skyline was to be seen. There was a foggy drizzle like on a November day in London; and we were nosing our way towards the Empire State building to the accompaniment of fog-horns.

I consoled myself with the thought I could now spend more time with the Press. I returned to my state-room, brushed my hair, filled my cigarette case with Lucky Strikes, and stuck a red carnation in my buttonhole. I then wondered whether I should stay downstairs or whether to sit up in the bar. Both were obvious places to find me—so I went to the bar.

On the way up I saw the reporters, who had come aboard by tug, bunched together popping questions at a grey-haired man in horn-rimmed spectacles. I wished they would hurry up. I had the same nervousness as an actor waiting for his entrance on the first night of a play. I chose a stool in the bar near to the door and, sipping a whisky, eyed the passage leading to it. Some minutes went by, and I had another whisky. Someone said we were passing the Statue of Liberty, and I got up and had a look at the green old lady. We left her behind and drew nearer the dock. Perhaps they've gone to my state-room, I thought. On the way

21

down I saw them on the stairs, cigarettes drooping in their mouths, hats on the back of their heads. They took no notice. They looked as if they'd completed their work for the day and were gossiping among themselves. I began to have a little doubt in my mind.

The steward was in my state-room, and I asked if anyone had been inquiring for me. 'No, sir,' he answered brightly, as if he were easing my fears that the police might be after me. I went back to the bar. I had two more whiskies, and chatted to the barman as if I were on top of the world. Someone said: 'They're swinging us into the dock.' I went out on to the deck and hung over the rail. Probably they'll see me on shore, I thought. And as I was thinking this, a passenger at my side laughed like a hyena. 'Did you see those reporters with their flashlights and cameras?' he spluttered. 'They were surrounding a little man who was the only celebrity they could find on the ship ... the great grandson of Lord Tennyson!'

2

I'd come prepared for a whirl of entertaining; to see the Rainbow Roof and dance into the dawn in Harlem; not to have one minute of the day to myself; to have a perfect stranger place his car at my disposal; to have more invitations than I could possibly accept; and, in fact, all those things I'd heard happen to foreigners arriving in New York.

22

I sent out twelve letters of introduction, and sat in my room waiting for the telephone bell to ring in answer. Though I'd flopped like a washed-up actress with the Press, it wasn't possible my introductions could fail me. Ever since the Boston tea-party it had been the fashion of the English to bury their faces in their hands with shame when comparing American to English hospitality. Here I was on certain ground. Yet the telephone was silent.

On the second morning the bell rang like an alarm clock, and I shot out of bed to answer it. A nasal voice drawled that he represented a news agency: 'We want to have the pleasure of taking your photograph. We missed you on the boat. Can we come now?' I was overjoyed that after all I hadn't slipped into New York entirely unnoticed, and I invited the gentleman to come round at once. For half an hour I posed; sitting, smiling, looking severe, standing. Then the photographer went away. Next day he returned with the prints, and after I'd admired them—he handed me a bill for five dollars. A well-known racket, I learnt later, of preying on the vanity of newly arrived foreigners.

On the third day, four more people took notice of me. The first was Russell Swann, the conjuror, who sent me a bottle of whisky; the second was Randy Burke, a delightful personality who earns his living inveigling other hotels' customers into the Waldorf

23

Astoria; the third was John Walters, an English journalist, who, on the fifteen occasions I subsequently lunched in his company, never once let me pay my share; and the fourth was an English friend of my family's, married to an American, who made me an honorary member of his clubs.

This attention improved my morale; but there were still eight other people whom I expected to take notice of me, and the fourth day passed without any of them doing so. It seemed I was playing the part popularly conceived to be that of the American arriving in London. I spent the day alone, sweating in the humid heat of my room, and the evening, wandering among the crowds of Broadway, Seventh Avenue, and Forty-Second Street.

On this fourth evening I was gloomily strolling back like an out-of-work undertaker to my hotel, when outside the entrance I saw a girl bending over a white Persian cat she had on a lead. As I drew near she stood up; and in the light of a street lamp, I saw she had fair hair falling to her shoulders, and a black dress without any frills, and no stockings on her slim legs. Her figure was like one of those in a film magazine, and her face had an arresting sadness with grey-blue eyes, and a lovely, generous mouth.

I went on for a few yards, then stopped, and came back. By the grace of God, as I drew level, the cat made a playful leap at my trousers, and all I had to do was to stoop quickly down, and seize the little beggar by the rump of its neck; and she was brought by the lead to within a yard of me. 'What's its name?' I asked sweetly, like an old woman asking the name of the Peke of another old woman. 'Dopey,' came the reply in a sharp, New Yorker's accent. 'And now you're going to bed,' she added; to the cat, not to me. She took it from my hands, and showing neither the green nor the yellow light, she walked into the hotel and left me outside.

I waited scarcely a minute before I followed her. I was the fox-hound within sight of the fox, and neither she, shyness, nor an earthquake, would swerve me from my quarry. She was sitting a few yards from the doorway with Dopey at her feet. In the light of the lounge she was more lovely than ever, hardly a touch of make-up on her face, and her hair in need of a comb, tumbling about her shoulders. A devil within me made me walk up unhesitatingly to her; firm and confident was I as I made the steps, but when I reached her I felt like the politician who dried up in his maiden speech in the House; I found myself standing there, muttering the horrid noises of a mute. No wonder she gave me no encouragement.

I didn't give up. I went over to the bar and gulped down a Bacardi; then with my nerves steady again, I went back into the lounge, and found Dopey had been handed to a page-boy, and the girl was walking across to the lift. This was the moment, now or never. I stepped quickly across the lounge, and stood between her and the lift-boy. 'Won't you have a drink with me?' I said; and before she knew whether she was standing on her head or her heels, I had my hand firmly on her arm, and was leading her to the bar.

That was how we met, Sarah and I.

3

Whether that was a good thing is open to question. I'd come to New York full of good intentions to write for my living and to record my reactions to New York life with the exactitude of a Pepys. After meeting Sarah, I did neither. My memory of the two months I was there is a jumble of red checked table-cloths in tiny restaurants off Seventh Avenue, sipping mint juleps in 'Twenty-One,' dancing to 'Always and Always' in the Stork Club, waking up at noon, and in the heat of the day exploring such diverse statues of New York as the Bowery, Rockefeller Centre, Battery Park, and Riverside Drive. There was the evening we went to the Palais de Danse on Broadway where five years before, when she was seventeen, she danced for ten cents a time. She was flat broke at the time, having spent the savings with which she'd left her home in New Orleans to find fame on the stage. But in the second week at the Palais she was walking down Forty-Third Street after the afternoon session, when a man stopped her. 'You're in luck, kid,' he cracked, 'Earl Carroll just saw you go by. He wants a word with you.' She went back with the man to where Earl Carroll was standing by the stage door of his theatre. 'Say,' he said, 'when the best pair of legs in New York walk by my theatre and they don't come in, I send after them, see?' Ten minutes later she had a job, and fifty dollars a week. There was the Sunday afternoon we swelted in Coney Island. The steamer from the Battery, jammed with negroes in straw hats, their women in bright red blouses, saucy girls hatless and bare-legged, men with cigars in striped linen trousers, fleshy women with moustaches. The shore black for five miles, with two million people swarming the sands like flies on bad meat. The barkers on Surf Avenue yelling into the microphones: 'See the four-legged man, ten cents!' 'Never before—the woman with the body of the bear!' Canned music. Burlesque shows; worn women in brassieres and slips. Screams of scenic railways. Peanut vendors: 'Take a large packet of delicious roasted peanuts, five cents!' Pineapple drinks. Jitterbug dance-halls. And all the rest that made the place a pandemonium. There was the day we saw Harlem from the top of a bus (ten years older than a London one) and watched negroes playing 'crap' on the pavements. The day we took a train to Long Island, and I found the same sandy dune country of the Belgian

27

coast. The evening we saw the first performance of 'Alexander's Ragtime Band' at the Radio City Music Hall, and out had to go my cigarette as smoking isn't allowed in American cinemas. And there was the evening we shot up to the roof of the Empire State Building, and from its dizzy height saw the fairyland of lights below us, and the neon signs blushing the skyscrapers into a purple darkness.

She was at the time playing the *ingénue* lead in a play in a Forty-Third Street theatre and, because she was in the minor ranks of the well knowns, I found myself getting the attention by being with her that I was unable to get by myself. John Chapman, for instance, in the *Daily News*, wrote a column about me, describing me as 'slender and eager' and beginning with the crack: '"I want to get away from it all—away from the cheap sophistication of the West End," Mr Tangye wrote in effect to his readers when he left. So he gets away from it all by landing at Twenty-One, the Stork, and El Morocco—and likes New York so well he fears he may get no further.'

And a few days later Louis Sobol, in his humorous column in the *Journal American*, wrote about the young British columnist who 'already has the problems of the world sitting on his back like lead weights, so he is taking a trip round the world and he will then write a book in which he explains how different people have told him what our purpose is for being in this world. The young British columnist does not expect to make much money from the book and the Queen says: "Heavens, I should say not. He would do much better just writing a book with lords and ladies in it and how they fall in love or, perhaps, he could make one of those British mysteries out of it." '

These paragraphs of nonsense tickled my vanity, but they brought work no nearer to me than the North Pole. But it did mean I met a few of these columnists, who become the more important, the more dirt they dig up. Chapman and Sobol are Puritans compared with their colleagues, and their columns are the more readable as a result; the others have the bounce, egoism, and conceit of Nazi *Gauleiters*, and swagger from restaurant to restaurant as if they'd earned the homage of the world. To one such little god I gave, at different times, five stories, each of which was good enough to lead his column; besides providing him with three letters of introductions to prominent newspaper men in London in view of his impending visit there. Hardly a word of thanks I got for my trouble, and his only effort to entertain me was a dollar dinner at a restaurant where he didn't have to pay.

They're as jealous as cats of each other, and pour forth mud on their rivals like women at a hen party. Since Walter Winchell is king of them all, it's like searching for a needle in a haystack to find a good word said in his favour. The night I met him it was so hot that in the Stork Club it was like dancing in an oven, so Sarah and I were sitting on stools at the bar. Ted Husing, the radio commentator, came up and suggested my meeting him; and we went over to the table in the corner of the room where he holds court every evening. He is a spare man, with thinning grey hair, a pinched face, and eyes that never keep still. He began his career as a 'hoofer' on the halls, wrote theatrical gossip in his spare time, and gradually climbed to being the Number One gossip writer of the world by making his news-dirt as witty in its way as an Oscar Wilde play. As I sat down at his table I gave a sop to his vanity by saying he was well known in England. He snapped back: 'By newspaper men, you mean?' I replied: 'Of course, but by the public as well.'

To my astonishment, without a trace of a smile, he roared to a few people at a neighbouring table: 'Did you hear that? I've got a big name in England. They like me there.' Then turning to me he said: 'It was *Wake Up and Live* that did it. God, what a wow that film was. Zannuck cleaned up on it.' I didn't ask why he hadn't followed it up with another. I didn't have a chance. He kept up a monologue of his achievements, and if in a pause I chipped in with a remark, he gave no appearance of listening. As I was launched in a sentence, he'd yell for a telephone to be brought to his table; or a telegraph form on which he'd scribble with the zest of a maniac. He was the epitome of the popular conception of an American newspaper man; and, let me add, he earns £18,000 for being one, and a further £30,000 for a weekly broadcast.

He is under contract to the great Randolph Hearst; and to young Bill Hearst, the son and heir, Randy Burke got me an introduction. He is a pleasant, well-mannered young man, whose office overlooks such a noisy section of Broadway that it's necessary to shout even in ordinary conversation. My idea was to persuade him to take me on as a guest reporter for a month; but in a quiet voice, quiet even if the office had been in the depths of the country, he explained that as his papers conducted a persistent anti-English policy, he couldn't in the circumstances employ me. That being so, I wanted to tell him the following story about his father.

Five years ago he was on a visit to England, and among his entourage was Miss Marion Davies, the film star. At the time he was in the palmy days of his life, when his fortune was estimated at £28,000,000. Since then, he's been what Hollywood calls 'on the toboggan'; newspaper after newspaper has been sold; his collections put up for auction; his salary cut from £100,000 to £20,000 a year; and most of his other manifold interests disposed of. He still inhabits his castle of San Simeon on the Californian coast, but it is on the scale of a Surbiton household compared with a few years back.

On his arrival in London, my editor sent me off to interview him. He was staying in a suite at Claridge's, and on going along there, I found him sprawling his bulk in a small arm-chair like the panda at the Zoo in a toy one. Miss Davies was there, too, and for an hour and a half I talked to the two of them; Miss Davies on her part describing the Billingsley painted Swansea china she had bought for St Donat's castle, and Mr Hearst, on his part, the chaotic mess in which he'd found Europe.

The interview over, I left the suite and walked down the hotel corridor to the lift. I hadn't gone ten yards, when I heard the pit-a-pat of footsteps behind me and the charming voice of Miss Davies: 'Hey, Mr Tangye, one minute.' I stopped, and found her beaming expansively at me. 'I wonder,' she said, 'if you could write a bit about me. The old man,' this with a jerk of her thumb over her shoulder, 'has been getting all the publicity this trip.'

I promised to do my best, and on returning to the office I wrote two stories, one about Miss Davies, one about Mr Hearst. Not unnaturally Mr Hearst's story was the more interesting, and the following day it was headlined in the centre page, while Miss Davies's story was omitted. I thought no more about it, but that same evening my editor received a telegram: 'Deny ever having seen your reporter. (Signed) William Randolph Hearst.' Ever since I've wondered what he meant.

4

If I'd been wise, seeing that I wasn't going to land a job, I would have left my Forty-Fourth Street hotel, taken an El down town, and found an apartment house off Seventh Avenue. Instead I preferred to play the part of a pseudo young man about town, and in doing so naturally spent too much money. The hotel room came to £2 10s. a week, and another £7 10s. disappeared on food and gaiety; this wasn't much compared with what I was doing, but I had to remember I was going round the world and had eleven months ahead of me. All New York restaurants have a bar where you can sit without paying a cover charge, though it doesn't stop you having the use of the dance-floor; so Sarah and I, by doing this, didn't have to spend more than ten or twelve shillings of an evening.

To begin with I felt ill at ease with her. I couldn't accustom myself to the accent and the slickness of her phrases. My ears were out of tune with language like: 'I've stood him up for a week,' or 'I'm giving him the brush-off,' or 'He has all the gall in the world,' or 'You'd better hock that watch.' It made me uncomfortable. She didn't, however, suffer from the bossiness which is the chief characteristic of American women. My own idea of an attractive woman is one who, besides physical beauty, has serenity, provocative innocence, and subtle changes of mood that mystify me; but American women, for the most part, are as bare of these qualities as the Serpentine of ice in midsummer. They have the brittle, forceful, competent manner of successful women business executives. They have screamed so long for equal rights with men that they have forgotten there was ever any reason to be proud of being women. Femininity is a forgotten art; they parade the world with the harsh, metallic spirit of careerists, disguised in slim bodies and lovely clothes. Homes and lovers are secondary in importance to the market they can make for themselves in frivolous society of the community centres, university clubs, and other women organizations which litter every American town. They rush at life like racing cars out for speed records, leaving no time for the lights and shades of living.

Nor could I accustom myself to the ease with which they get drunk. 'Drunkenness to an American girl,' said a French born night-club proprietor, 'isn't bad manners or vulgar. She looks at it in the same light as smoking too many cigarettes.' This seemed indeed to be

34

true. I never went to a restaurant in New York, San Francisco or Hollywood, high class or low, which by midnight didn't have among its customers several women (any age from seventeen to seventy) who were as drunk as their male escorts. If they had been just merrily tight, one perhaps wouldn't have minded, but they drank so hard that that stage never lasted for long; they were soon noisy and bawdy, and rolling about the dance floor like music hall drunks. Maybe you're thinking I am exaggerating. I assure you I'm not. In my first week in Hollywood I saw three glamorous film stars, whose names are on everyone's lips, being carried out of La Conga, Clover Club, and the Brown Derby, in such a state that they couldn't have known whether they were in Hollywood, Bournemouth or Pago Pago. Still odder was the number of girls in their teens whom I saw in the same state. Can you imagine seeing an English débutante in her 'coming out' year flopping about the Mayfair like a Saturday night drunk, as you can see an American débutante in the Stork Club in New York or in the Mark Hopkins in San Francisco? When I voiced my disapproval to an American, he replied: 'Oh heck, you English are so darned reserved. The kids are only showing *joie de vivre!*'

5
I did succeed in flirting with work. I got £5 for

an article on Barbara Hutton, and another £5 for one on the Duke of Windsor. With my usual optimism, for these two thousand word efforts, I'd expected three times as much; but once again I'd overestimated American standards. Unless the article is syndicated or you have a big name, you're paid less than in England. And as far as the working journalists are concerned, their pay is twenty-five per cent lower than reporters of corresponding standard in London; that, of course, is always excepting the top-flight men who earn astronomical figures.

Two other articles I wrote were eventually published in England. One concerned the Consumer's Union, an organization which protects the man in the street from being duped by advertisements. For 12*s*. 6*d*. a year an American can receive a Buying Guide issued by the Union which gives the truth about every product in the market. Take for example toothpaste. All the brands are classified under three headings; 'Best Buys,' 'Also Acceptable,' and 'Not Acceptable.' Only two brands are listed under 'Best Buys,' another two under 'Also Acceptable' and the rest under 'Not Acceptable'; among the latter are most of the best-known ones. One brand which advertises on every other hoarding in England is said to be 'excessively acid. There is some indication that this toothpaste may have harmful solvent action on the tooth enamel.' Another 'will not whiten teeth as claimed. Price excessive.' All kinds of goods are classified in the same way: coffee, tea, silk stockings, beauty creams, face powders, canned foods, cold cures, motor-cars, cameras, radios, etc. Research into the products are carried out mostly by university professors so as to ensure impartiality. Their accuracy must be 100 per cent or the Union would be deluged with libel suits; as it is, in the eight years of its existence, it hasn't had one. Despite this success, newspapers won't have anything to do with it; they see the possibility of their biggest advertisers being run out of business, and rather than that they'd prefer to have the man in the street spending his money on dud articles.

The second article I wrote described a visit to Sing Sing prison. It's a five cent, half-hour train journey from Times Square. I was ushered into the deputy warden's office just in time to hear the end of a telephone conversation concerning some fellow's reception into the death-house. While he talked, I went over to the window, and looked at the prison buildings sloping down the hill until they were stopped by a high wall, the other side of which was the main New York—Chicago railroad. Spaced at hundred yard distances, I could see three watch towers on the wall, each round like a lighthouse; and against their railings there lolled warders, rifles in their hands. Then further away was the vast width of the Hudson River, seldom empty during the day of the little steamers that puff the two hours' journey from Battery Park so that tourists, with field-glasses, can gloat on the prison from afar. I turned back to the warden. He'd finished his call. 'That fellow I was talking about,' he said, 'they had him up for two killings. He was freed on the first, but they've got him on the second. He's due in the death-house tomorrow, where he'll stay till he goes to the chair.'

I sat in the chair myself ... the officer who was taking me round, thinking it a funny joke to push me in it. Somehow I'd expected the death-room to be modern, designed like the inside of a modern cinema; chromium plated, plush seats for the witnesses. Instead, I found it low ceilinged, with dirty yellow wood panelling, and three wooden benches of the same colour in one corner; and the chair, in the centre of the room, was a derelict object of rusty steel and dark leather straps. It was like a scene in a Frankenstein film, and I was glad to get out of it.

Star prisoner on the occasion of my visit was Richard Whitney, ex-president of the New York Stock Exchange, who is serving five years for fraud. His cell was one of a block of five hundred. It was about ten feet by five and had a bed, a wardrobe, washing basin and WC. One end was a small grilled window, the other was a barred door, opening on to the landing where the warders walked up and down, day and

38

night. He had no special privileges (he had wireless headphones of course like the rest), and his job in the prison was to teach visual education to fellow prisoners who were too simple-minded to learn any other way. In the cell next to him was a negro who was serving a life sentence for cutting his sweetheart's throat.

The men wore grey flannel trousers and white shirts; and as it was the lunch hour when I made my tour, many were lounging in the sun. As we passed they would touch their caps, saying 'Good afternoon, warden.' He was at pains to explode the idea that the prisoners live a life of ease and luxury. They work eight hours a day. They are not allowed to have food sent in from outside, though they can have a ration of cigarettes. They can have five visits a month from relatives, each lasting an hour, and they can have a letter a day. Certainly, it is more enlightened than any of our British prisons, but in the few hours that I was there, I didn't see any evidence of the wild stories of easy living I'd read so much about.

6

The day following my visit to Sing Sing, there was a line in the Broadway column of the *New York Daily News*, saying: 'Derek Tangye, round the world reporter, can't tear himself away from New York on account of a gal in *Silent Music*.' I had, however, already made up my mind to leave; and I had bought a bus ticket for San Francisco, costing only £8 for the three-thousand-mile journey. If I went through non-stop it would take five days, but I was able, if I so wanted, to stop over at any place on the way. The bus left its terminus in Forty-Second Street one Friday evening at eight o'clock. I remember it was raining so heavily that, though my hotel was only a few hundred yards away, I had to take a taxi to escape being drenched. It reminded me of that gloomy, wet night I'd arrived in Manchester, six years before, to begin my career in journalism, and I had the same depressed and lonely feeling as I had then. Sarah could not be there to see me go, as she had to be at her theatre; but when we had said goodbye she gave me a letter which she made me promise not to open before midnight, when I would be many miles away.

Midnight came. We were careering along at fifty miles an hour across New York State. Jersey City, Clinton, Belvidere had come and gone. I was huddled in the back corner seat, the fabric of the bus on one side of me, a gross German on the other. The lights were out, and I had to read her letter by the light of the moon that jerked its rays through the window.

Please don't be angry with me [I read]. I'm giving you this instead of a cigarette lighter or some other silly thing you'd have no use for. Every bit helps and I'm sure you can use it. Besides, it's very easy to carry and won't

40

take up any room like a book. If you send it back to me—I'll elope with the first man I can find.

Out of the envelope, on to the coat warming my knees, dropped a ten-dollar bill.

CHAPTER THREE

HIGH ROAD TO 'FRISCO

Throughout the night, I was jerked from side to side in the back seat of the bus. Every place was occupied. Beside me was the gross German engineer on his way to California. His fat face would fall first on my shoulder, then on the shoulder of the man the other side of him. In the seat in front of me was a mouse-like little woman who slept peacefully, until I brushed her head while putting on my coat. She awoke with a start, swung round with fists clenched, and demanded: 'Did you hit me?' Every two hours the bus stopped. The lights were switched on, and we had ten minutes to take a walk. At five-thirty in the morning we pulled up at a café somewhere in the Alleghany mountains. A gramophone was blaring dance music from a window. The driver drawled: 'You have thirty minutes here, folks. Early morning breakfast.' Fried eggs and coffee cost

41

1*s*. 6*d*.; then back we scrambled into our seats, the women with faces lined and greasy, the men collarless with stubble on their chins. Off we careered to Warren and Erie.

I gave up hope of sleeping. If I rested my head on the ledge beside me, vibration jarred it like a pneumatic drill. We charged along, as the morning grew hotter, at fifty miles per hour through wooded valleys, past white-washed villages left behind in a cloud of dust. I wondered what would happen if we crashed. One safety door was at the back, the main door was by the driver's seat. The windows were too small for anyone to squeeze through. A nigger strummed a guitar, humming 'Dinah'. The German opened conversation: 'Just come back vom Hamburg. Does England vant var?' Fifteen minutes for lunch. A shilling for corned beef hash. The drivers changed. 'So long, folks,' said the parting one. 'Howdee,' said the new one.

Here was Cleveland. Euclid was the name of the main thoroughfare; on either side of it were sumptuous houses with lawns sloping hedgeless to the sidewalk; and on the fresh green grass were wooden placards, with the words 'Funeral Home.' All over the States, funeral homes are thriving, go ahead businesses, but never did I see so many as on that afternoon in Cleveland.

Something was wrong with the wheel of the bus. Out we clambered, and my two suit-cases

42

were shoved in another. Then on to Toledo. The road lay beside Lake Erie. The curl of a steamer's smoke on the horizon. The lake, grey like a dull day on the English Channel despite the blazing sunshine. A cloud of flies flew in through a window; up jumped a little man, ten days' growth of black beard on his chin, with the ears of a mule and the eyes of Mussolini, who swiped at them like a maniac. The same little man, when we got to Chicago, said to me: 'Whatcha think of sharing a room, cheapa yer know!' We entered Chicago eleven o'clock Saturday night. For an hour before we halted at the bus station, we passed factories ablaze with lights, mile upon mile of them. Black porters in red caps queued up to take our luggage. The German was going on. He had thirty minutes to wait, and then into another bus. No one could have induced me to do the same. I went to the first hotel I could find, had a bath and slept twelve hours. The next morning a gale was blowing old newspapers down the streets. Chicago didn't seem very inviting. The sidewalks were deserted and my hotel empty. A bus was leaving for Omaha at one-thirty and I decided to take it. This time I knew the ropes; I was smart enough to get a seat in the fourth row, where the springing is smooth enough to read a book. The seat tipped backwards and, having hired a pillow for ninepence, I was just as comfortable as sitting in a train. It was the same routine as from New York to Chicago.

43

Ten-minute stops every two hours. Mile upon mile of flat, dusty country. My fellow travellers changed at each stopping-place. First was a traveller in ladies' underwear. He was a thin man with a few fair bristles as a moustache. He had the harsh accent of Ohio, and he spoke with a vehemence that suggested that any argument he was engaged in would be very one-sided. His subject, strange then to my ears but which afterwards I heard spoken of quite often, was revolution in America. 'I get around in my job,' he said, 'I go places and hear things. Take my word for it if there's a war in Europe there'll be revolution here. Here's how it'll happen. You've heard of the Nazi Bund which Mayor La Guardia frequently attacks? They represent the German minority here, and everyone knows they're hand in glove with Hitler. If the fire flares up over there and there's talk of us coming in they'll flood key points of this country with arms. Already they've got arsenals all over the place. Get the idea? It won't matter to them who gets the rifles. Let the Communists do the rest of the dirty work. Hitler'll be satisfied if the civil war that breaks out keeps America from helping the democracies. You wait, that's what'll happen.' He got out at Sterling, Illinois, before I could hear any more.

Darkness was falling, but at intervals summer lightning painted the plains a silver white. The bus was air conditioned, but the

44

night too was cold. I put on my overcoat and buttoned it round my neck. Ten minutes at Ogden, a hamburger sandwich and a cup of coffee, and we settled down for the drive through the night. I couldn't get to sleep, a drainage inspector prevented me. He was a massive man with a small, thin voice; he had a red tie and double chin; and his body overflowed irritatingly into my seat. 'Say, is that so?' he piped good-naturedly when he learnt I was English. 'I've got an uncle living today in Greenock.' (All Americans, incidentally, have an uncle or aunt living in England, Scotland, Norway, Italy or Germany.) It transpired that this gentleman was an employee of the WPA, otherwise known as the Works Progress Administration, the corner stone of the New Deal. It is the biggest industry in the world, employing around 3,000,000 people and paying out £1,000,000 a day in wages. It is Roosevelt's pet panacea for unemployment. His enemies attack it on the grounds that the country cannot afford to support the system indefinitely, that he is using it solely as a vote-catching machine, and that it is being run on lines that are wasteful, inefficient, and corrupt. That is the propaganda they're pouring out to the Little Man of America. The drainage inspector, however, seemed to be unmoved by it. 'They say the country can't afford the WPA,' he said, 'well, let them tax the wealthier

45

classes a bit more. Do you know the average income of persons with £200 and more is taxed less by half than any country in Europe? Mind you, I don't think the WPA is run efficiently—yet. But everyone is in such a hurry. It is only six years since the first WPA worker got his first wage. The Standard Oil wasn't built up in that time—and the WPA is bigger still. I'll tell you one thing. There are a heck sight too many employees of the WPA who are feathering their own nest. Out and out corruption. But that's because we haven't got a class of people like I believe you have—I mean the civil servant.' He paused. Then added: 'Anyhow, what's the alternative? None of the guys who want to run against Roosevelt have a better plan. Even if they said they had you wouldn't believe them. Compared with Roosevelt they're all either ignorant hicks or political crooks.'

Spasmodically I slept through that night. At six we were rumbling into Omaha, chief cattle town of the Middle West, but no one was about; in the half hour we were there I had a wash and a shave. Then we were off for Cheyenne. We weren't tearing along as we did in the Alleghany Mountains, Nebraska had a strict speed limit, and we crawled along at twenty miles per hour. Level to us was the main line to Los Angeles and San Francisco. First there thundered past the 'City of Los Angeles'; then, later in the afternoon, the yellow painted

'City of San Francisco'. Soon after, rain began to fall in torrents. In half an hour the road was a foot deep in water. We were passing Kearney, a village of wooden houses, and as we splashed into the open road a man stopped us with a red flag, warning the driver the road was giving way. 'Thanks, highwayman,' drawled the driver. We moved on slowly. On the railway track, little motor-driven trucks sped along the line, jammed with workmen. After every downpour they inspect the track in this way. As the weather cleared, we set off again at our twenty miles per hour through the Wild West grassland to Cheyenne. I'd intended to drive through the night to Salt Lake City, but in North Platte a red-haired, tipsy old woman got in. For four hours, amid hiccups, she maintained a monologue on the history of her family. Her grandfather was a parson, her father a sailor, her husband a bricklayer, and her son was serving a sentence in Kansas City gaol. 'Not that the polooka deserves it,' she croaked. She was to be tolerated while she sat at the back of the bus, but shortly before Cheyenne she saw a vacant seat behind mine. Over she came, and with her, a smell that suggested she hadn't washed for some months. She began stroking the back of my head. 'Turn round, handsome,' she said. 'All right, sweetheart,' I answered, 'but keep your hands to yourself.' I was thankful when we pulled up at the Cheyenne bus station half an hour later.

The first thing I saw, as I stood on the pavement, wondering where the hotel might be, were three figures clattering past me on horseback. A street lamp lit them up, and I saw the spurs on their long boots, and their high cupped saddles. For the first time in my life I'd seen cowboys. I went into a bar, and found men hunched round the tables throwing dice, in yellow, red, blue shirts, wide cowboy hats, and khaki riding breeches. Each wore an ornamented belt, and one mean-faced little man, lolling against the bar, was waving his belt in the air. 'Yellow rat,' he cried boastfully, 'you have to go far south to get that!' He, like most of the others, was drunk. I accidentally knocked into one. 'Get out of my road,' he murmured. I started conversation with another. 'Sounds like an Englishman,' he said, 'well, well, you're the first one I've ever met ... Howdee!' He caught my hand in an iron grip. Then he added slyly, with a wink to his comrades: 'But don't think we're ever going over there again to pull your chestnuts out of the fire.' Everyone, including myself, roared with laughter. 'If you get yourselves into trouble,' he went on, 'that's your affair, not Uncle Sam's. We came over to save you last time and what did we get? Nothing except a lot of money you've never paid us.' We talked in this vein for a while, and when we were becoming a little heated, I bade him farewell and went off to the hotel. Next morning I was in the bus again at eight. We passed mile-long cattle trucks, travelling even slower than we were. We saw 'hoboes' perched on the top, and they waved at us as we went by. Nowadays they're allowed to 'jump' goods trains without fear of being ordered off by the railways' police. We were leaving the plains and climbing into the boulder country of the Rocky Mountains. Several times we passed herds of wild horses. We saw them silhouetted against the skyline, standing head to head, flapping their tails; or galloping away from us through the dry pampas grass.

My neighbour was a broad, dark-haired man of thirty, dressed in a dirty grey shirt and creased corduroy trousers. Every so often he burst out in a bass voice into one of Verdi's arias. 'I'm going to be a great singer,' he explained in a slow Middle Western drawl, 'for ten years I've been studying. I'll study for another five and then'll make my début on the concert platform.' He had indeed a fine voice; he had also a whisky bottle in his pocket. He took gulps at it every ten minutes, and towards evening it was nearly empty. By this time he was encouraging the rest of the passengers to sing, but not very successfully, as his own voice was loud and by now out of tune. Suddenly the bus stopped. The driver left his seat, and made his way up the aisle to where my friend was sitting alongside me: 'Gimme that bottle,' he snapped. 'Can't you read?' He pointed to a

49

notice: 'No alcohol in this bus.' My friend spluttered apologetically, made one or two more efforts to rouse the vocal enthusiasm of the rest of us, and then subsided into a drunken slumber.

It was too dark to see the scenery of the Rockies. There was no moon. I could only tell that we must be pretty high as for two or three hours the bus had been in second gear. At last it went into top; and the driver casually over his shoulder said: 'Continental Divide, folks.' Henceforth the rains and the rivers drained into the Pacific. For three more hours we coasted downhill towards the Utah Desert through Evanston, Morgan, Ogden. I dozed awhile, and when I awoke we were driving through the broad avenues of Salt Lake City. It was midnight and the streets were empty.

Salt Lake City is, as you know, the headquarters of the Mormons. I myself didn't know any more about the religion except that I believed they practised polygamy. And when I awoke next morning, the first thing I did was to look out of the hotel window and see how many chimneys the house had on the other side of the street. I had the idea that you could tell the number of wives a Mormon possessed by the number of chimneys in his house, each chimney denoting the private room of a wife. I was fifty years out of date. I saw neither a house with an unusual number of chimneys nor did I meet a Mormon with more than one wife.

50

Polygamy ceased in the 1880s when the United States passed a law forbidding it, and the president of the Mormon Church, John Taylor, received a revelation from the Lord ordering him to obey the law. The Mormons, I therefore found, were ordinary people. I found, too, that they were a practical people. In addition to the ritual of their faith, they face earthly problems such as unemployment. The Elders have put into practice a scheme in Salt Lake City which has cured unemployment as far as members of the Mormon Church are concerned. No Mormon is allowed to accept Unemployment Relief; instead they are guaranteed work. They are allotted jobs according to their capabilities and their desires; and if certain of them aren't physically strong, it's seen they aren't given heavy work to do. The Elders believe that what can be done among a population of 100,000 can be done elsewhere on a far greater scale.

The inhabitants of Salt Lake City are by no means all Mormons; and the most successful paper, the *Salt Lake Tribune*, is a Catholic-owned organization. Half the day I was in the city I spent at the service of this paper. I accepted the offer of the news editor to write a column on my impressions; and I praised the wide streets, commented upon the many pretty girls, and remarked how willing everyone was to help a stranger. The article stretched down a column of the page with a grinning picture of myself at the top, so I presumed what I wrote was satisfactory. But I scratched my head and wondered—the only sign of hospitality or reward I saw during my stay of thirty-six hours was one Virginian cigarette.

I left at eleven in the morning and was in Reno twelve hours later. It was a monotonous journey of five hundred miles across the alkali desert of Utah and the sage-bush country of Nevada. The bus's air-conditioning apparatus had broken down.

It was stiflingly hot; it wasn't any use opening the window as dust blew in like a snowstorm. At Elko, a strange fellow got in whom I'd seen twice before on the trip. Each time he'd got out at a small hamlet, once about an hour's ride outside Omaha, and another time at Laramie near Cheyenne. He had a grey drooping moustache, a pinched face of reddish complexion, and the watery eyes of a heavy drinker. Though his back was hunched and round, he was still tall, so that in his young days, fifty years ago maybe, he must have been a fine-looking man. At one of the halts he was sitting next to me in the café, so I mentioned I'd seen him before. 'Yes,' he answered, 'I've been two weeks on this journey from New York, hopping on and off. I get bus-sick, you know. My heart begins to beat in jerks. It doesn't get normal till I get my feet on firm ground. I've to take my luck where I get off.' We got back in the bus together and he sat down beside me, pulling out his pipe. We were riding through the Tuscarora Range; for miles it would be flat, then we'd see an isolated hill, sticking up out of the plain like a man's fist.

'Indian country this,' said my companion, 'out over there in the bush is a big reserve. If a white man wishes to trade with them, he must ask the Chief first, treating him with the respect of his position.' He knocked the bowl of his pipe on the heel of his shoe. 'I was married to an Indian girl once,' he said suddenly in his slow drawl. 'It was a long time ago. Texas was my home state and I worked on a ranch of Captain Ogilvie. He and the Indians got on fine, which was strange, as there were always shootings and goings-on in the ranches around. I did a bit of trading with them on my own account, liquor for furs, and so on. And that was how I came across "Star in the Night," that was the translation of her native name. Pretty, isn't it?' I nodded. Darkness was falling and the driver had switched on the headlights, beaming the road white before us. 'She'd just turned sixteen,' he went on, 'and no one so lovely have I ever seen again in my life. Black eyes like the night, and a body with the litheness of a gazelle. I, a lad of twenty, fell head over heels in love with her. I saw to it that I traded pretty frequently in her village. The Chief saw, too, my reason. Mind you, I hadn't touched her. If I slept with her, I'd have had an arrow in my back within twelve hours. I had to have her legally, according to white man's law, if I were to have her at all. Finally I asked permission of the Chief to marry her. My pals said I was crazy, but I didn't care. I'd decided I couldn't live without the girl. So I went to the Chief, a fat old devil he was, and do you know what he said? In his vernacular, of course: "You can have the girl ... but give me first six bottles of whisky"!' My friend rocked with laughter at the memory of the occasion. He threw back his head and roared. 'What about the girl?' I asked, when he'd quietened down. 'Oh, she,' he replied, in a tone of voice as if signifying the unimportance of my question, 'she married me, but she couldn't stick it ... After a year she went back to the village.'

Reno wasn't far away. We climbed into hills and down again, round hairpin bends to the valley that lies at the foot of the Sierra Nevadas. For a mile we ran along a boulevard which surprised me with its respectability. Solid three-storey houses like those of Kensington. But then we crossed a level-crossing and encountered the real Reno; stretching across the street above us were these words in lights: 'The Biggest Little City in the World.'

There doesn't seem to be any point in this announcement. Maybe it's because every house in four streets is either a night-club or a gambling-house; and in another part of the town there's licensed prostitution. As one official put it to me: 'You can't do anything wrong here, we make it legal.' The gambling-houses have no doors to their entrances. They're open day and night; and the Bank Club, the chief one, has its entrance paved with silver dollars. The players are a motley collection. You find sleek, Schiaparelli dressed women sitting side by side with 'desert rats,' the uncouth, mining prospectors of the mountains. They play roulette, faro, poker, blackjack, chemin de fer and keno; you'll find the stakes are anything from 6*d.* to £1000.

Women predominate among the intending divorcees, husbands apparently can't spare the time off for the six weeks' residential qualification; so you see them in droves, gloomily playing the tables or being gigoloed in the nightclubs. While waiting for the divorce, they describe themselves as 'taking the cure,' and having got it, they talk of 'winning my diploma.' Mostly they stay the six weeks on a dude ranch which is the same as an ordinary ranch without its discomforts. The cabins are steam-heated, with electric light, and the food is cooked by French chefs. Handsome cowboys are there, too—usually impoverished New Yorkers dressed to look the part. The cost of staying at one of these places is between £25 and £70 a week. The cost of a divorce slides up and down according to the complications of the alimony settlement. From £50 to £5000. Two hundred and fifty lawyers practise in an area of one square mile: today they're worried because Reno divorces are on the decrease while marriages are on the up; last year there were three thousand divorces compared to eight thousand marriages—and a marriage costs only £1 for the licence.

Jack Cartwright, the publicity manager of Reno, told me that on no account should I leave town without seeing 'The Crib'—the home of licensed prostitutes. The local police have it nicely ordered. The women are registered at the police station where they're told the regulations: not to talk to men beyond a certain street, to submit to a weekly examination, and to ply their trade only in 'The Crib' where they pay the police 2s. an hour for the use of a hut. The police also provide them with whistles in case the visitors are unwelcome. I paid them a visit; to enter 'The Crib' I passed through a gate where I was scrutinized by a police officer. Commenting to me upon his work he said: 'Prostitution in the States is either a gangster or political racket. We prefer to have it on a sensible basis.' Forty-odd huts were built in a horseshoe shape round an open space. Peering through the windows and the doors were a score or more Jezebels, old and revolting. They lured me with their cries of: 'Come on, darling.' I talked to a couple for two or three minutes, and when they saw I wasn't a customer, they lost patience. 'Why don't you go up town where you belong?' one

56

of them snapped. Excusing myself I said: 'I don't belong up town. I'm broke.' Hiss came the reply: 'Scram, then ... or I'll blow my whistle and the cop'll bag you!'

I was indeed broke. I'd left New York with £3 in cash, and I left Reno with 3*s*. I wouldn't have had that, if Jack Cartwright hadn't invited me to stay one of the two nights I was there. San Francisco, where a Letter of Credit was awaiting me, was twelve hours away, and I had meals to pay for. The road wound up the pineforested mountains of the Sierra Nevadas, passing lakes cupped in the valleys, and log cabins designed to look from the outside like those of the Wild West days, and in the inside the best the twentieth century can offer. We were half-way to the top when the bus stopped. Here was the state line dividing Nevada from California. We waited five minutes, then a black-shirted policeman in a peaked cap popped his head inside. He had a quick look round to see if any one of us was an escaping criminal, and then departed. We were only a dozen, and none looked a potential criminal except a wizened little Chinaman in the seat in front of mine. He had been sitting impassively with his hands on his knees all the way from Reno, and he continued to do so until we were nearing Sacramento. Then, apparently, the change of temperature from the cold of the mountains to the heat of the valley upset him; for he was violently sick. I pulled down the window beside me, trusting the wind would blow the stench away; even so I needed a gasmask. An English woman, employed as a dress designer in New York, was in the seat behind. She had travelled five days non-stop from New York, and her resistance was low. One whiff of the Chinaman was enough for her. She also was sick.

At Sacramento, thank heavens, we changed buses; and off we went on the last lap. Once again the country for mile upon mile was as flat as a pancake, but this time instead of the desert and the sage bush, as far as the eye could see, was golden corn. At Sacramento it was stickily hot, but the nearer we drew to the coast the colder it became; and when we were within an hour of the journey's end I had my overcoat on, buttoned up to the neck. It grew darker, too, and though it was only six when we reached the tramway lines of Oakland, it was a race of minutes whether night was to fall before we touched the Bay Bridge.

The night won, and all I could see, after we'd passed through the toll-gate, was the spatter of lights through the holes of the girders; high and low they were, against the background of San Francisco. What magic in that name! Somewhere in those hills of stars were the places that for so long had stirred romance and adventure in my heart ... Barbary Coast, the Embarcadero, Chinatown, Fisherman's Wharf. And away from them, on the right of me, half-way to the Golden Gate that was part of the darkness, was the island of Alcatraz, only a handful of lights as the signpost of its whereabouts. I sat there, fascinated, staring into the night, oblivious of my companions who were collecting their baggage.

The bus pulled up at the terminus in Market Street, soon after we'd left the bridge. As always, negro porters scrambled to take our baggage. I took no notice of their persistence, and, giving up the last slip of my ticket to the driver, I began to lug my two suitcases to an hotel a hundred yards down the street. A cold wind cut my face and bare hands, like March in England, not September in California; and I was glad to reach the warmth of the hotel. I staggered to the reception counter and booked a room. But as I signed my name, I saw out of the corner of my eye that the hotel porter had taken charge of my suitcases. He would not hand them over to me, and up in the lift he went, and along with me to my room. He put them side by side in a corner … and then waited. He stood like a rock. He wasn't going to let an Englishman get away without a tip. But he was wrong. There was nothing else I could do. I hadn't a cent. I went into the bathroom and locked myself in.

CHAPTER FOUR

CALIFORNIA, HERE I AM!

I'd spent precisely £100 since the day, ten weeks before, I'd set foot in New York. It was necessary to economize. I decided to allow myself £25 for the following month, and to stay in San Francisco. For four days I tramped up and down the hills that are so steep that the tramcars are run on cables; and finally I found an apartment at the corner of Sacramento and Stockton Streets on the edge of Chinatown. The rent was 30s. a week, for which I had a sitting-room, bedroom, kitchen, and bathroom. It meant I had a little under £5 a week for food and pleasure, which wouldn't go far if I found myself paying for a round of drinks with a single whisky at 1s. 9d. and a beer at 1s.; and if I mixed with the people with whom I wanted to mix this was certain to happen. One of these people was Gertrude Lawrence who was playing in *Susan and God* at the Curran Theatre. This was pleasant for me, as it meant that on arrival in 'Frisco, I did at least know one person; but it also presented the problem of expense—one evening might see the end of £2 or more. I kept away from the theatre for a few days and wondered what I should do. Obviously this money problem was

60

going to become more and more acute, especially when I landed in Hollywood. It was the old story of 'keeping up an appearance'. Look prosperous and you'll get around. Appear as if money is scarce and you'll find yourself alone. The inhabitants of California, I was told, particularly followed this dictum. I had, however, a long way to go, and I'd no wish to squander my funds. Suddenly I hit upon an idea. I would tell Gertie, and anybody else when it became necessary, that I had lost £200 of my travelling expenses in three nights' wild gambling in Reno; that I was obliged, by what I'd said in my article, to stay away for a year; and that if I were to do so I had henceforth to exercise the strictest economy. The story was an instant success. People thought it gloriously funny. And for the rest of my travels I brought it out whenever I was threatened with expense beyond my means.

2

Gertie was a phenomenal success in San Francisco. She played five weeks longer than she was scheduled, faced queues of fans every night after the performance, and had her activities splashed daily in the newspapers. No actress for fifty years had received such a welcome in the city. Gertie was quite unmoved. She went serenely on, greeting everyone with the warmth that made them go home the first time they'd met her and say: 'Gertie told me

61

this...'; while she herself forgot their names and everything else about them. She'd wear her lovely clothes, waltzing out of her dressing-room looking incredibly smart, planting a kiss on Eddie Cooke, the seventy-year-old manager of the show, and lilting: 'Cooky, darling ... only six dollars in the bargain basement!'—and the next evening wear something fifty times as expensive. There'd be a party every night and she would sing for us—but never 'Someday I'll find you' because: 'I've sung it out of tune often enough.' Authors would come with ideas of new shows and she would give them all her attention; delighted especially with one of Johnny Green's whose 'Body and Soul' she first sang (she had bought a half-share in the royalties for £50) because she explained: 'Darling, the curtain goes up and there I am on a bicycle with my bottom to the audience!' She'd talk of Noel Coward: 'I have never known him any better from the day I first met him to this.' She'd appear vague and charming, but she'd catch you out if you contradicted something you'd said twenty minutes before. She'd go to bed at three, but be up rehearsing a new play at ten. She'd find the maximum of pleasure in the minimum of amusement. One evening she and I were taken on a tour of Chinatown by the Chief of Police. We ate chop suey with chop sticks, walked down dark alleyways and up rickety staircases; and pretended all the time we were risking the dangers that haven't existed in the district for fifteen years. A British warship happened to be on a courtesy visit to 'Frisco, and towards two in the morning we saw three able seamen swaying slightly in the middle of Grant Avenue. They affected both of us with nostalgia for home, so up we went to make their acquaintance. By way of introduction, Gertie, in her delightful confident way, with the words going up and down in the scale, said: 'I am Gertie Lawrence!' We waited in suspense for their reaction. 'I am Gertie Lawrence,' repeated Gertie, 'you know ... the actress!' They looked at her a little unsteadily; then one of them mumbled: 'Well ... if you are ... ssshow ush where we can get shome women!'

It was lucky for me that Gertie and those with her play, were in San Francisco because they lightened by their presence an otherwise uncomfortable month. Hitler was up to one of his tricks and I spent a great deal of my time listening to the radio and buying newspapers and getting angry with Americans for calling Britain 'yellow'. In addition, there was a crisis in the city itself, in the form of a retail store strike. You couldn't walk down the street without passing ten squeaking females with banners announcing: 'This store is unfair to organized labour'; and if you entered a store which was being kept open by a skeleton staff, you ran the gauntlet of a hissing picket of men and women. Their demand apparently was not the question of wages nor the length of working hours; they were on strike because they wanted to control the selection of employees. For fifteen years San Francisco has been bothered by strikes and the effect on the general atmosphere is noticeable; it was strained; cab drivers, waiters, shop salesmen were sullen and unobliging; there was none of the romance and irresponsibility that I'd expected. The longshoremen have been on strike so often that shipowners have lost patience with them; and if they aren't on strike they deliberately slow their work so as to collect overtime pay. It's no wonder that fewer and fewer ships call at 'Frisco, and instead make Los Angeles the chief port of call on the west coast.

After two weeks I realized I was being even less of a success than in New York. I was ready to admit that it could be my fault, but this could hardly be so when letters of introduction weren't answered; even though the recipients were in town to receive them. I was puzzled, too, why just ordinary politeness was as rare to find as a fly in midwinter. On my third evening in the city I was invited to a charity ball at which the *élite* were predominant. I imagined that it would be an excellent opportunity to get to know people, but, after being there three hours, I had talked to about a score of Americans, all of whom addressed me in monologues, without attempting to draw any

64

conversation out of me. And when it so happened that I was talking to one by the bar, more often than not, it was I who paid for the drinks, not the American. One man did invite me to lunch the following day, but when the bill came, he said he was sorry he had forgotten his money, so I had to pay!

3

I would have gone after two weeks if it hadn't been for the fact I'd rented my apartment for a month; and the remaining two weeks were no better than the first. Much of it I spent in bed; I also wrote some articles for the *San Francisco Chronicle*. In the evenings, if I wasn't at the 'Curran Theatre', I lounged about the bars and cafés of North Beach, downtown of 'Frisco, the district of the old Barbary Coast and Chinatown. Not that these places are any more of interest. By day Chinatown is a spick-and-span shopping centre for the tourists who roam Grant Avenue and Sacramento Street, gazing wide-eyed at the hieroglyphics that decorate shop signs; and by night it welcomes the tourists again, the cafés with whisky and respectable Chinese waitresses, the streets and alleyways with guides who, in addition to their fees, beg for a donation on behalf of their suffering cousins overseas. It was in one of these cafés that I did, however, meet a girl whose companionship brightened a little the monotony of the days.

65

Her name was Penny. She was eighteen with a figure like that of Ginger Rogers; and her way of living was to show it clothesless three times a day, along with six others of her sex who were nearer forty than thirty, to an audience of sailors of all nationalities, and an assortment of tired business men. She was a chorus girl in a burlesque show. The programme of these entertainments consists of a film with a title such as 'Dangers of the White Slave Traffic', a ten-minute interval when the programme seller urges you to buy a picture book ('but don't look at it now or your neighbour will blush'), and a variety show of vulgar comedians with Penny and her friends.

She had been in 'Frisco two years. She had come down from Seattle where her father was a longshoreman. She hadn't ambitions. She said she was too small for ordinary chorus work. All she wanted was to stick around 'Frisco and earn a living. She didn't really mind standing naked on the stage, though 'Saturday nights are a bit rough.' She liked to laugh; also to cut dates with me. Her favourite drink was hot chocolate and she enjoyed walking along the shore by the Pacific. On the whole she had very little to say for herself; but there was a freshness about her that was as delightful as it was unexpected.

The evening before I was leaving for Hollywood, I'd met her after the show and we'd walked down Vallejo Street to Leoni's, where Leoni, a swarthy little Italian who hated Mussolini, had asked me for a farewell drink. A halfdozen American sailors were lounging against the bar, and another was at a table with two flashily dressed women on either side of him; four other tables were filled, three by a nondescript collection of men in black Trilby hats playing dice, and one by a taxi-driver. It was plain that this gentleman was drunk. His cap was on the back of his head, his green shirt was open at the neck, and he was wailing a song that had no tune to it. We'd been there five minutes before he recognized Penny; then with a whoop like an Indian war cry, he rose unsteadily to his feet with a glass of beer in his hand, and swayed over to us. He was a broad, unshaven hulk of a man with a jaw that stuck out aggressively. Leoni had a hunch that trouble was coming because he darted round the counter to play the part of a nurse remonstrating with a disobedient baby. The taxi-driver, or Ed as he introduced himself, pushed him aside, and leeringly complimented Penny on her performance. 'Do yer act now, shister,' he spluttered. The sailors were roaring with laughter. The men in the Trilby hats stopped playing their dice. 'Do so yourself, buddy,' cracked back Penny. For some minutes Ed continued to persuade her to oblige until he had become, in my view, a nuisance. Then it was that I was foolish enough to say something. I think it was: 'Perhaps you'd

67

better go home now, Ed, old man.' Anyhow, he swung round to me, repeated what I said in an exaggerated English accent ... and threw his glass of beer in my face.

Two of the sailors grabbed my arms and two others grabbed his; and while I was held there, he was protestingly pushed outside. I saw Penny go, too, and when Leoni came back a few minutes later, she wasn't there with him. The sailors, pleased with themselves for having so promptly stopped a brawl, had let go of my arms and I was mopping my face with a handkerchief. 'Where's Penny?' I asked. Leoni paused for a second. 'Say, bud,' answered Leoni, 'that guy Ed is Penny's boyfriend ... she's been standing him up ... that's why he was sore.' He went behind the bar. 'She's taking him home,' he added, 'and she told me to say thanks and wish you luck.'

I never saw her again. At six o'clock next morning I was in the Greyhound bus, bound for Hollywood.

4

That same evening I was strolling down Hollywood Boulevard with Miles Mander. Dusk was falling and it was hot, like an August evening in Regent Street in a heat-wave. An hour previously the bus, after an uneventful journey, had dumped me down in Cahuenga Avenue, where Miles was there to greet me and take me to the Mark Twain Hotel. I went

68

through the ceremonies of signing my name and finding my room as quickly as possible. I had the naive excitement of a schoolgirl in my desire to have my first glimpse of the city. Nor was I disappointed.

Hollywood, as everyone knows, sprawls over many square miles; MGM studios are as far from Warner Brothers as Piccadilly Circus from Watford, and there is no break in the lines of houses separating Hollywood from Los Angeles. But it is in the one mile of Hollywood Boulevard, from Vine Street to Grauman's Chinese Theatre, that you see the highest concentration of Hollywood beauty. It is not the beauty of the film stars, they are in Beverley Hills and the villas off Sunset Boulevard, but the beauty of the extra girls that are waiting for their call to fame. Blondes, brunettes, redheads, in scanty shorts and slacks of orange, white, pink, and blue. Scarlet lips and dark sun-glasses. Figures of Cochran Young Ladies. Painted toenails, sandals and bare legs. On that first evening I saw score upon score of them, perfect examples of that synthetic beauty that is the fashion of the world. And as I stared and marvelled at this cavalcade of sex appeal, I heard Miles say: 'Don't get tied up with these lovely animals. They'll cost you a fortune and you'll get nowhere.'

Circumstances forced me to take his advice during my month's stay. Night clubs are dotted over an area of twenty miles, and as American

69

girls can't sit still in the same restaurant for more than an hour, it would have meant spending in taxi-cab fares alone what would have amounted to an ordinary night out anywhere else. In any case, these extra girls must be seen in the right places where there's always a hope of a director spotting them or a successful film star taking a fancy to them. They are all waiting for the Chance; and, strangely enough, a good many of them have their mothers waiting with them. They've trekked into Hollywood, the mothers basking in reflected glory, from Missouri, Minnesota, and Texas, after winning the local beauty competition; without brains, talent, or influence, they imagine a miracle will speedily put their names in lights, and even after the first months of disappointment, they still believe with incorrigible optimism that the Chance will come, next week, next month. One such mother and daughter were living in my block of apartments. They'd been waiting eight years and the daughter's bloom of youth was fading. But mother was undaunted. One evening as I was walking upstairs with her, she confided: 'Our little girl Hortense is sure going places some day.'

I wrote an article about the lives of these extras, and to help gather the material, the Central Casting Bureau sent me three girls to interview. The Bureau provides the extras of every film made in Hollywood. Eight thousand men and women are on the books, and only in special circumstances nowadays is anyone else signed on. They are divided into four classes; the £1-a-day class, which is so far from the camera that it doesn't matter what anyone wears; the 30s. class, for which a girl needs two evening dresses and a man a dress-suit; the 45s. class, for which a girl must have four evening dresses as well as smart walking clothes; the 75s. class, for which is needed the wardrobe of any smart man or woman about town. The Bureau keeps a check on the earnings of all the eight thousand, and the result is interesting. Last year four thousand earned more than £150; one hundred and twenty-six more than £400; sixteen more than £500; and only three more than £600. The rest of the eight thousand earned less than £100. Against these figures, you have to bear in mind the cost of clothes. A girl whom I saw, who had earned £650, told me her wardrobe was insured for £1500. It consisted of twenty-four evening gowns, several fur coats and wraps, twenty-five pairs of shoes, and ten sports and street clothes. They have to be in the latest fashion or directors won't want them. She told me that she pays out an average of £2 a week to keep her wardrobe in condition and to pay her hairdresser, and the cost of transport to the studios. Seems hardly worth it, especially when you learn that out of forty-five thousand people registered with the Central Casting

71

Bureau in the last twelve years, only sixteen have got their names into bright lights; Clark Gable and Janet Gaynor being the prime examples. Two other girls I saw were the kind that danced and posed in the mammoth musicals of two years ago; so now that Busby Berkeley is out of fashion, they are out of a job. In 1936, a boom year for them, they earned £600 each, but in 1938 they were lucky to get a £100. They shared a flat off Highland Avenue near the Hollywood Bowl: they cleaned the flat themselves, cooked their food, and made their own clothes. Any day, however, it was on the cards they'd be called up to play the part of a sophisticated glamour girl. They were hard little realists. The youngest, aged twenty-one, said: 'Sure I've tried being kept by a guy but it wasn't much fun. I'd to run around like a hired motor car. There's more kick in being independent.' The other, a year older, blue-eyed and blonde, cracked: 'Six years in this racket and you're a sucker if you sleep with a man before he gives you the job. Sleep a night with a man and he forgets next morning what you slept with him for. "Nuts," I say when they make a pass.' Then she added a little thoughtfully: 'Maybe it's different with the big shots.' Both of these girls talked about the Chance that one day would come their way. Heavens knows how. But they talked of it like you would talk of the plans you're going to make next Christmas. Hard boiled careerists;

you can't help feeling sorry for them and the hundreds like them.

Miles Mander has a disarming manner of apparent indifference to his runs of good and bad luck. He has an attractive air of irresponsibility and an attitude of carelessness towards matters which other people make much of. Today he is having greater success on the films than ever in his career, but for a couple of years in Hollywood he frequently didn't have enough to pay his rent. When after a long bout of unemployment he did succeed in getting a big part, he collapsed on the set on the very first day of 'shooting', and was taken to hospital. It was found advisable to operate at once, but the doctor first asked him if he had any money to pay for the fee. Miles, who was semiconscious, didn't answer; the doctor rang up the bank. The bank said Miles had five dollars. The doctor came back: 'We won't operate, Mr Mander, until you get someone to guarantee the fees.' Miles (he was afterwards on the danger list for fifteen days) roused himself from his semi-consciousness to tell the doctor what he thought of the American medical profession. He then phoned Madeleine Carroll, who dashed round half an hour later with the money.

It was a strange coincidence that the man who had the part before Miles was Jameson Thomas, the English star of silent days, who also collapsed on the set seriously ill. He was a great friend of Miles's, and knowing Miles was in need of a job, managed to get a message to him that owing to his illness the job was vacant. Jamie Thomas, though I met him only twice, cut a picture in my mind that I'll never forget. His young wife died in California of tuberculosis, six years before he himself was struck down with it. He had for long been out of work, and he had no money to pay for proper treatment. The Motion Picture Relief, however, came to his aid, paying for a bed in a sanatorium at Sierra Madre, on the outskirts of Pasadena. It was here that I met him, lying haggard and unshaven, in a room whose window faced a wall and where he saw no sun. He had many friends who were wealthy and who were ready to help him, men like Ian Hunter and Ronald Colman, but he was too proud to accept their charity. He wanted them only to bring books which he afterwards returned. None of his friends remember him complaining, but in his last three months he talked always of England. He was being given some sleeping drug which made him dream vividly. He told me that he would dream so vividly of his young days in England that it would take him two or three minutes when he woke up to realize where he was. And then, unconsciously speaking the truth, he used the expression: 'I'm dying to see England again.' But he died there in that little room whose window faced a wall and where he saw no sun;

and his friends will remember him as a man who radiated a fineness that made them feel it had done them good to have known him.

5

I had my fill of stars. One of the very great, on an introduction from a mutual friend, gave me lunch with his wife and a famous director. I'll always remember that lunch because, no matter what I said, no one took the slightest notice. Obviously, it was a bore having to ask me to luncheon at all and, once there, why should they bother to make conversation with me? They prattled along about their own affairs and gossip: 'I refuse to play opposite Claudette Colbert'—'Did you hear that one about the Bradna girl?'—'Jack caught Claire in bed with Bob,' and so on. I got so annoyed that when the coffee came, and after I'd made another meek attempt to make my voice heard, I rose up saying: 'I'm very sorry I must go now. I'm playing golf with Groucho Marx.' Then, for the first time, they took a look at me. I was worth their attention. Not that I had ever met Groucho Marx in my life. A more pleasant lunch was with Loretta Young. This took place in the studio restaurant of 20th Century-Fox; the tables filled by yellow-face-powdered men and women in garments ranging from modern evening dress to crinoline frocks of the nineteenth century. Loretta herself was in a crinoline of violet and lace frills, looking demure with big round eyes, and teeth that don't look so prominent as they do on the screen. Just as I arrived at the table where she was sitting, Doc Bishop, who was introducing me, was called away, leaving me stranded. Loretta smiled sweetly. 'Do sit down,' she said, 'my name's Young.' The most shining example of modesty I've ever met.

The same day, Harry Revel, the song writer, took me along to see Shirley Temple. He walked me across to her bungalow in the studios, where we found Mrs Temple sitting knitting on the doorstep. She is thin, dark-haired, and fortyish. 'Oh Harry,' she said, getting up, 'a whole lot more letters saying Shirley's a midget.' Harry told me later she gets frantic about some of the letters sent to Shirley; she insists on reading all the fan-mail. To me, however, she seemed a sensible woman, the sort of housewife who would always buy the best value at the cheapest price, and a woman who had the pleasant habit of appearing interested in what you're saying. As we were talking, Shirley, earner of £1000 a week, appeared through a doorway. She was in a white party frock, with white socks and shoes. Her hair had a reddish tinge and her eyes were a deep brown. Mrs Temple glanced at her: 'Shirley,' she said firmly, 'you've got a smut on your nose. Go and wash it off before you shake hands.' Shirley obediently turned and went into the bathroom. The following day I was watching her play a scene with Anita Louise. It happens that she is obliged by law to spend a certain number of hours every day learning her lessons; and after each scene she goes to her teacher who times by a stop watch how many minutes she puts in before the next scene is ready. When this particular scene with Anita Louise was over, Mrs Temple cried out: 'Hurry, Shirley ... school!' Shirley pouted her lips and sighed: 'Ooo ... that word haunts me night and day!' It was this same afternoon that I had my picture taken with her. Obviously, Miss Temple didn't want to have hers taken. She sulkily came up beside me, her head reaching my waistline. I wondered what to do to soothe her ruffled feelings. I felt oddly embarrassed, as if the Queen was unwillingly doing me a favour; but I didn't know whether to make my peace with a child of ten or with the Queen. As it was, I looked glum, imagining the grim little face below me; but I shouldn't have worried, Shirley is too well trained—when the picture appeared she had on her face a beaming smile. She redeemed matters for me a few days later, after I had pushed her several times up and down on her swing, by enrolling me as one of her police; as she pinned the imitation gold medal of office on my coat, she remarked gravely: 'If ever I catch you not wearing it, you pay me a dollar!' The last time I saw her, she was sitting by herself in the back seat of their limousine (Mrs Temple always sits in front beside the chauffeur). They were just moving off for home when Shirley suddenly said: 'Oh Mummie, I've forgotten Dinah, can I get her?' and out she scrambled to fetch her doll.

I found it reasonably cheap living in Hollywood. I paid £2 a week for an apartment in Wilcox Avenue off Hollywood Boulevard and in four weeks I only spent a little over £25; this, however, wasn't achieved without effort. Many evenings I sat at home wishing to goodness I could go out; yet to do so would probably have resulted in my spending in one night what I'd budgeted for a week. To go out alone could be all right, as I would linger a long time over one drink; but as like as not I would meet somebody and then it would be drink for drink and away the money would fly. There were some to whom I could admit my state of affairs; Guv Charlot, for instance, who to the loss of the English stage now lives in Hollywood. He and I used to sit on stools in La Conga and watch the girls and boys enjoy themselves. Myrna Loy with a shiny nose and dressed like a pleasant, homely housewife. Alice Faye enjoying absinthe. Joan Bennett dancing cheek to cheek with Walter Wanger. Jean Parker liking whisky. Tables of rowdy parties. Guv himself had just finished being technical advisor to 'Zaza' and he had no idea what he was going to do next. For that reason he would never go out of his apartment by day. He said he had to stay by the telephone in case a producer rang him up. Most people pretend, as I myself was doing, that they either have more money than they've got, or that they're more successful than they are. Guv preferred to joke about his position and go on smoking his cigars and playing his contract bridge at 6d. a hundred. Once I did hear him say: 'It takes grit to be cheerful'; and there was another time when I was talking about the value of prestige. He answered: 'Never rely on prestige, it's the facts of the moment that count.' So now Guv, who gave first chances to Ronald Colman, Jack Buchanan, Gertrude Lawrence, June, Jessie Matthews and a host of others, is waiting to get a chance himself.

6

I got weary with being shown round the studios. Architecturally all studios are the same; the stages, the research department, the wardrobe department, the music department, the carpentry shop, the laboratories. The publicity men insist on showing you everything, and by the time I'd seen 20th Century, MGM, Warner Brothers, Paramount and Radio, my adjectives of praise were worn to shreds; because, obviously, you have to praise each studio above another. The publicity men must have been more bored than I was, but they didn't show it. They placed cars at my disposal, entertained me to lunch, offered free tickets at previews, introduced me to Mickey Rooney, Clark Gable, Spencer Tracy, Adolphe Menjou, Franchot Tone, Joan Crawford; and with the fuss of an art dealer showing me a Gainsborough, one of them let me look at a screen, the other side of which Hedy la Marr was having a bath.

The classic tour of Hollywood studios was made by Cedric Belfrage. Cedric, as anyone knows who has read his books, is a rebel against convention. He writes what he feels, being quite indifferent to the possibility of his remarks bouncing back unfavourably on him. When he was a film critic, he was in perpetual hot water with the film companies. They didn't think they deserved his outspoken criticism since they were paying considerable sums for advertisements in his paper; and especially angry was MGM who, for a long time, wouldn't have anything to do with him. When, however, Cedric went to Hollywood for a month, MGM thought it time to patch up the quarrel; and they decided to do it in a big way. Cedric was invited to lunch by Irving Thalberg, then head of MGM, who afterwards personally conducted him on a tour of the studios. For two hours Thalberg talked to Cedric, while the publicity men hovered in the background quite certain that Cedric had been won over by this honour. But they were wrong. Cedric's next article attacked Thalberg for wasting time—he said that a £100,000 a year man should have something better to do than to be a guide to a £20 a week journalist.

MGM have never forgiven him for this; and in other studios one also doesn't often hear pleasant things said of him. They're scared stiff that at any moment he may lash out on them; especially that now he has made his home in the Santa Monica mountains where he lives with his small daughter Sally, and his wife, Molly Castle. Molly and I were wheeled in our prams, side by side, on the promenade of Blundell sands. Today she is undoubtedly the best English woman journalist, and her Hollywood articles in the *Daily Mirror* the most readable ones of their kind. It was principally due to the two of them that I had such a good time in Hollywood; they spared no trouble so that I might see all that there was to see, and meet not only the blah film stars, writers and directors, but also the others who resemble the normal intelligent people found in any other city in the world. And through them, I met the first American who lived up to my expectation of American hospitality ... George Volk, the agent, who loaned me his car, invited me to stay with him, entertained me and took endless trouble giving me introductions to various highups in different studios. There were many other people who made me feel that Hollywood welcomed a stranger; or at any rate, gave him a chance to find his feet before passing judgment upon him.

But scarcely had I found these friends than it was time to move on. I was going to Tahiti.

For a long, long time I'd had my South Sea dream, a picture in my mind of sighing coconut trees, and gentle blue lagoons whose tranquillity would bring a balance to my thoughts and a peace I could not find elsewhere. In my teens, I measured happiness by money, pretty girls and holidays. I imagined that if I had the money to take out a pretty girl and a holiday during which I could do so, I would be forever content. One day, when I do not know, it suddenly came upon me that there was something vastly more complicated which ruled my happiness; and that, to achieve it, I had to find my way through a labyrinth of doubts and fears, until all at once, like coming upon an oasis in the desert, I found myself with peace of mind.

Tahiti, it had seemed to me, would be that oasis; ever since I'd read Rupert Brooke's letter of farewell. 'I was sad at heart to leave Tahiti,' he wrote. 'But I resigned myself to the vessel, and watched the green shores and rocky peaks fade with hardly a pang. I had told so many of those that loved me, so often, "Oh yes, I'll come back—next year perhaps, or the year after"—that I suppose I had begun to believe it myself. It was only yesterday, when I knew that the Southern Cross had left me, that I suddenly realized that I had left behind those lovely places and lovely people, perhaps for ever. I reflected that there was surely nothing else like them in the world, and very probably nothing in the next, and that I was going far away from gentleness and beauty and kindliness, and the smell of the lagoons, and the thrill of that dancing, and the scarlet of the flamboyants, and the white and gold of other flowers; and that I was going to America, which is full of harshness and hideous sights, and ugly people and civilization, and corruption, and bloodiness, and all evil. So I wept a little, and very sensibly went to bed...' His words had caught my imagination, and in the years since I'd read them I'd woven round Tahiti my dream of escape, believing that, if by some lucky chance one day I was able to go there, life would become again as simple as when I was a boy.

The difficulty was how to get there. There were two ways: one from San Francisco by a cargo boat which sailed every six weeks, and the other by a French passenger steamer which passed through the Panama Canal from Marseilles about as often. Unfortunately, the cargo boat was booked six months ahead (it only carried ten passengers), while the French boat was booked up for two months. I was told, however, that if I took the risk of going down to Panama I might be lucky and get a cancelled passage. The risk seemed to be worth taking. I could not imagine myself, once there, not getting aboard. Meanwhile, I had to get to Panama. I wanted to go via Mexico and Central America, but I found there was no regular train or bus service after the Mexican border, and the only way was to go by boat from San Pedro.

And so, on one sunny Monday morning at midday, I boarded the Norwegian steamer *Takanar*, with eight days sailing ahead of me, five days in Panama waiting for the French boat, and then, I hoped, fourteen days across the Pacific to Tahiti.

CHAPTER FIVE

PANAMANIAN INTERLUDE

The 'Takanar' was 8000 tons, loaded with lead, zinc, fresh fruits and lumber. She had come down the west coast from Vancouver, calling at Portland, Seattle, and San Francisco, before San Pedro; and after Panama she sailed across the Atlantic to Southampton and Liverpool. She did this trip four times a year, there and back, and very seldom was she ever in her native country of Norway.

My cabin was on a small deck directly beneath the bridge. It had a berth with a spring mattress, a wash basin with a cold water tap, a wardrobe, a sofa which would have been another berth had it been occupied, and two windows facing the bows; to reach it I had to walk through the small smoking-room where there was a wireless and three tables and a half-dozen chairs, which were fixed to the floor, so that if the weather was rough they would not slide about. There was room in the boat for eight passengers but this trip there were only three aboard. One was an ex-Canadian civil servant retiring to England, another was a young prelate on his way to be ordained in Panama, and the third was a South American bishop. For eight days we were thrown together, with the same intimacy as if we'd been wrecked on a desert island.

The civil servant was named Harris. He'd been alone on board for a fortnight, and no sooner had we cast away from the dock and were heading for the Pacific, passing far away to our left a squadron of American warships anchored near San Diego, than he buttonholed me and unleashed all his unspoken conversation that had been boiling up inside him.

I learnt that he suffered from heart trouble, had had all his teeth taken out, had lost 45 lb in six months, had been 20th in the King's Prize at Bisley in 1908, should have had a pension after the Boer War but was cheated out of one, that he had lived by himself in Vancouver, and was going to stay for the rest of his life with his brother at Bristol. When I told him I'd been to

Hollywood, he said: 'That's the place where they make films, isn't it?' and went on to explain how he'd been to a number of films in the previous few months but couldn't remember the names of them. 'Know the stars though,' he added cheerfully. 'Myrna Low, Tyrone Powell, Loretta Faye.' The bishop was Spanish. He spoke a burbling broken English, little of which I could understand; and he ended every remark with a twitch of his black eyebrows and a giggle. The young prelate had the name of Figaro. He had the head of a guinea pig, with large flapping ears and a pair of black, beady eyes. He told me he had been studying at 'Crompton,' and he said the word 'Crompton' in such a tone of voice that I felt sure I should have known it as I do Paris or New York.

The four of us had our meals with the Captain in the oblong dining-room, which in daylight was darkened by the lumber, piled high on the deck outside. The Captain was a pleasant, round-faced little man with bushy fair eyebrows. He hadn't been to his home in Norway for more than two months in eleven years. His last visit had been three years ago, and during that holiday, he told us, he had married. Coyly he said, in halting English: 'I have not seen my wife since.' There was an embarrassed pause, all four of us thinking of the poor little wife; and it wasn't broken till the bishop, with no reference to any previous

86

conversation, began telling us a tale how he'd once seen a whale off the coast near New York.

After supper I stood on the fo'c'sle listening to the swish as we cut through the water. The sun was setting, and it was very still. To starboard was the glow of the dying sun, pink and gold; but ahead of us was the jet blackness of a thunderstorm. It stretched from the faint line of the Californian coast far into the Pacific Ocean, and we were sailing into the centre of it. The blackness would be suddenly shot with jagged fork lightning or the black clouds would turn grey by a flash like the summer lightning of England. I thought we were in for a big storm, but it melted away as we drew nearer, and only a few spots of rain spattered on the deck. I felt lonely as I stood there, and a little homesick. I thought of the people whose friendship I had shared in the past few months; only to move on, leaving them behind. I thought of Sarah who had telephoned me from New York the night before I sailed; and, as the sun dipped behind the horizon, I wondered whether I would ever see her again. I thought of my mother and father, and the months ahead of me before I would be with them again. I had an acute desire to hear their voices, and, if there had been a telephone aboard, no matter what the expense, I would have put a call that moment through to England. There were many times in the year I was away that I felt like that. I would arrive at some city in which all were strangers; but without fail long letters from my mother and father would be waiting for me; and there was one evening, when I was sitting in my room in Hollywood, when the telephone rang, and I was told London wanted me. I didn't believe it—but a minute later, as clearly as if it had been a local call, I heard my brother Colin's voice. He just wanted to know whether I was enjoying myself. I knew then, even if I hadn't known before, that I was lucky in my family.

2

At meal-times, on the table in front of the Captain, was a dark-coloured cheese which I learnt was goat's cheese and a speciality of Norway. For some days no one partook of it except the Captain, until one evening Mr Harris, who was proving himself a bit of a wit, announced in frolicsome mood that he was going to take some. I offered to do the same, saying: 'I won't let you die alone!' With Figaro laughing and the Bishop grinning as he stirred the bread he had stuck in his coffee, Mr Harris and I each cut a microscopic piece and with great play proceeded to sniff it. Unhappily we had been taking no heed of the Captain; for he had taken exception to our behaviour and, speaking slowly and deliberately with cheeks flushed a deep crimson, and his broken English more broken than ever, he said: 'Thaaat ees foood yooo arre eeeting. Thaat's nottt tooo beee sneeefed aat!' We tried to smother our laughter, like choirboys in church, and Mr Harris turned to me, whispering: 'We've insulted the national cheese!' Even Figaro and the Bishop were laughing, and it was painful to see the hurt look on the Captain's face. 'Eeet's verrry goood cheese,' he added plaintively.

But a much worse scene was to follow. The afternoon before our arrival at Balboa, the Pacific end of the Canal, where I was to disembark, I went to my cabin to pack and discovered that forty-five dollars I had left in my suitcase had disappeared! I went exhaustively through all my belongings and then got Mr Harris to do the same. I knew that once I mentioned it to the Captain there would certainly be a row. He would naturally consider I was casting aspersions on the honesty of his crew. When, however, Mr Harris found nothing, I went to the Captain, explaining that it was no doubt my fault, that the notes must have caught in the leaves of the book I was reading and, having fallen out, got blown away. He, in his turn, searched every shirt, every envelope and everything else in my two suitcases. And, as he too found nothing, it was embarrassingly necessary to call for the steward. He gave no help; and that evening we had dinner in a subdued strain. Afterwards we went upstairs to the smoking-room, the Captain to play chess with the Bishop, and I to talk with Mr Harris. We had been talking for about ten minutes about my misfortune when the Captain, apparently overhearing us, banged his fist on the chessboard and stood up. 'Mr Deerek,' he said sternly, 'eef yoo vaant too hearr vaat I'm theenking, eeet ees thees. I veeel tell yooo thaat I theenk yoo neverr haad thee money!'

Now this moment required great calm. I sympathized with the Captain over the position he was in, but here he was accusing me of stealing my own money. I made no answer and he went on: 'But too keep yoo quiet, I, a haard-vorrking maan, veel pay you thee forty-five dollars out of my own money.' The Bishop, with hands clasped and elbows on the table, was staring at the chess-board. Figaro was intently reading a book. Mr Harris had stood up, watching me. 'Thank you very much,' I said to the Captain, 'but beyond that I will say nothing until you've apologized for what you've accused me of doing.' And with that I marched off to my cabin. Once there I saw the humour of it, and also the seriousness; I was left with two dollars sixty cents and my bar bill unpaid. It upset me, too, that the Captain should have his pride so hurt, and when he arrived to say he was sorry, I assured him again that I blamed only myself; though I realized that this couldn't be of much satisfaction to him. We said goodnight on friendly terms, so that when I got up next morning I expected we would be able to discuss the situation more

90

calmly. But this, however, was when the Bishop stepped in. As we sat down to our porridge, amid many a giggle and a twitch of his eyebrows, he made these remarks: 'This is the end of a voyage, so let us make new resolutions ... we will not be careless ... we will not drink too much ... we will not lie!'

The incident had an extraordinary sequel. That morning everybody went through my things again, without any luck. But two months later, when I was in Tahiti, I was looking through my suitcase, and I found, neatly folded in the corner of the suitcase, the whole forty-five dollars! How we missed it I will never know. Nor why it was that I didn't find it for two months, because almost daily in the meantime I had been unpacking and packing that same suitcase. I wrote off immediately to tell the Captain.

3

I landed at Balboa with my two dollars sixty cents knowing that I had to get to Colon, the Atlantic port of the Canal, where a Letter of Credit was waiting for me, before I got any more money. Figaro and the Bishop landed, too, and were met by a covey of clerics who made such a fuss of them that when I went up to bid them good-bye, the Bishop only gave me a nod. Probably he judged me as a sinner, but surely, I thought, here was a chance for him to do a bit of saving. He and his clerics, I saw, had

91

five cars at their disposal; he knew that I was going to the station, and he knew that I had no money; in his infinite goodness he might help the sinner on his way. I hung around for a while, but so much bowing and scraping was in progress that no one noticed me and my two suitcases, hopefully watching. It struck me that if they were to see me struggling along the road, especially if I were in the middle of it, they could not fail to stop; so off I started lagging the wardrobe of a year's travel with me. The Balboa station was only a mile away, but the heat was such that you could have steamed a steam pudding on the pavement, and sweat poured from my brow as if I were taking a shower-bath. Added to my misery, shiny black negroes offered to be my porters at thirty-second intervals, and couldn't for the life of them understand why 'the white fellah' shooed them away. I had gone perhaps seventy yards when a toot behind me warned me of the coming of their reverences. Obstinately I stuck in the middle of the road. More toots. The first car was directly behind me, so I turned to face it, exhaustion written all over my face, heaving my suitcases at the same time to the side. There was His Grace in the front seat, his black eyebrows directly facing me; a faint smile of appeal lit my face, but the man was unmoved; the driver pressed the accelerator and away they went. One, two, three, four cars hurried in their wake, but the occupants were too occupied with themselves to worry about the traveller on the wayside.

The ticket cost two dollars forty cents, which left me with twenty cents to spend in the five hours before the train was timed to go. Balboa was no place to stay, there was nothing more exciting than a few shipping offices; so, having left my baggage at the station with instructions to have it put on the train, off I went on a five-cent ride in a 'jitney' to Panama City, about ten minutes away. By this time I was parched with thirst and, on being dropped off in the square, I spent a further ten cents on a coca-cola; this left me with five cents which quickly became two when I bought a newspaper. I had four and a half hours before me, so, with the buttons of my shirt undone and my coat on my arm, I started to sight-see. No sooner, however, had I begun walking up the main street, past the windowless shops, than I found everyone in Panama had something to sell. It was amazing. After thirty yards I found I'd collected a procession, a rabble of Indians and negroes, pestering me with Panama hats, lottery tickets, souvenirs, bathing costumes, and a mass of other articles. Worse was to come. I managed to escape down a side street and found what appeared to be a lonely bench. I sat down to read my paper. I had read no more than the headline when a dozen little black boys appeared from nowhere, each with his shoe stool and his cry:

'Shoe shine, mister!' The difficulty was that my shoes obviously needed a shoe shine. They were the shoeshine boy's dream, muddy and shineless. I pretended they were not there, but that only made their cries the louder. So I said sharply: 'Run away, little boys, run away!' Peals of laughter greeted this. A couple got on the seat beside me. 'Only five cents, mister ... only five cents!' I was at my wits' end. It was impossible to cope with such persistency. Frankness was the only way out. 'Listen, little boys,' I said, 'it's a long story and you wouldn't understand it even if I told you, but the long and short of it is that I'm broke ... not a dime ... not a nickel.' And with that I rose from my seat and made for the station. I was both weak in body and bad in temper when finally the train came in. To my luck the purser of an American passenger liner sat beside me. He didn't waste time with words of introduction. 'Have a swig,' he said, proffering me a half-bottle of whisky, 'plenty more where that came from.' I looked at him with astonishment. 'I've read about people like you in books,' I said. 'What part of the States do you come from?' 'My home's in Carolina,' he replied. 'Ah,' I said, 'the Southern States ... I only went to the east and west.'

Next morning, having slept the night at the Hotel Washington in Colon, an expensive but clean hotel run by the American Government, I visited the offices of the Messageries

94

Maritimes. They told me that the *Ville d'Amiens*, my boat to Tahiti, was not expected for another four days, but, in any case, they said, it was useless my thinking I could get aboard her; they'd just received a wire to say there wasn't a vacant berth on the ship. The news was damping, but it made me the more determined. I told the clerk that I didn't mind how I travelled, in the stoke-hold or the engine-room, anywhere, so long as I sailed to Tahiti. He was a nice little man with a head too big for his body; I departed from him with the arrangement that I should return in three days and, meanwhile, he promised to cable again to the ship.

Colon, if possible, is one worse than Panama. The town straggles unnoticed into another called Cristobal. Colon is under Panamanian jurisdiction, and Cristobal, which is in the Canal Zone, under American. In both, America is supposed to enforce sanitary ordinances, but most streets are slums with a stenching odour of open drains in the sultry, humid heat. The clerk at the bank said on my first day: 'The drains have a bad smell this week because it hasn't rained for some days.' He spoke as if he were explaining why the grass on the lawn had dried up. He didn't seem perturbed. Walk down any street and you see the downstairs living-room of the negroes opening doorless on to the pavement. The bedrooms, ceilingless, like stables. Women and children squatting over basins. Aged gramophones screeching Spanish melodies, no music in the jarring, maddening tone. Children running around in the roadway with black, bare bottoms. Girls sauntering along with thick purple lips. Barbados negroes swaggering with exaggerated waists. Old men limping with jet-black faces, their unshaven faces grey with stubble like mildew. And at night American soldiers from the garrison and sailors from the fleet jam the bars and dance-halls. Panatropes blaring their fox-trots, making the night seem even hotter. Naval police in brown gaiters and white tunics marching through the bars. Military police in wide-brimmed Scout hats swinging thick canes patrolling the streets. Colon ... where a glass of beer costs 2s. and a whisky 3s ... where meat tastes like leather, and the hairdresser charges an extra shilling for putting brilliantine on your hair. I never wish to spend five days there again.

The one bright spot of my stay was an evening with Tyrone Power. I'd met him three or four times in Hollywood, and the last time I'd seen him, in the Clover Club the evening before I left, he told me he was due in Panama about the time I would be there; he was taking a flying holiday round South America. Sure enough, on my second evening, he flew in from Mexico City and rang through to my room (he was staying in the same hotel) within a half-hour of his arrival. We just had time for a drink before he rushed off to make a couple of personal appearances, but we arranged we should meet afterwards at the Atlantic Club.

The Atlantic is the Café de Paris, the Rainbow Roof, of Colon. Night after night it seethes with sergeants, able seamen, corporals, petty officers, of the American Army and Navy. The bar and its tables open on to the dusty pavement of Bolivar Street, and the passers-by are tempted inside by the pretty girls, especially imported from New York, that are sitting around waiting to be their hostesses. They are, however, respectable young ladies. The boss of the Atlantic has to deposit a £100 bond with the authorities for each one on arrival; he gets it back so long as there's been no scandal around her name when her contract is up. They live in dormitories above the club which they get free. They also earn 25 per cent on all the drink they persuade their partners to buy, and as the cheapest is 3s. 6d. they don't do so badly.

I was having a drink with one of the girls when Ty Power came in. He looks more manly than he does on the screen, and he has an effortless and charming manner. He takes his success as rather a joke, and it doesn't appear to make him feel any more self-important than if he were a bank clerk. As he stood beside me he was attacked by autograph hunters, and I noticed the way he fixed his charm on each one individually as he signed his name, rather than on the whole crowd as most celebrities do. We got away from them after a while and sat at a table that sided the dance-floor. Every inch of it was jammed with hugging couples. The swing band of negroes yelled and screamed their rhythm. Military police passed to and fro between the tables. Sailors, in their white linen jackets, sprawled over their chairs drunkenly making love to their girl friends. Cigarette girls with bare legs and short skirts sex-appealed their wares; and heat and smoke palled over the room like fog in a monster oven.

We'd been there five minutes when he saw a girl he wanted to dance with. 'That girl over there in a white dress and a red rose on her shoulder,' he said, 'do me the favour of asking her to dance and bringing her over here.' He then explained the drawbacks of being a film star. In his unknown days he'd played the sport of picking up girls. He'd see a pretty little shop-girl and think it a pity he didn't know her; he'd conceive some original way of making her acquaintance, and if he were snubbed ... well, he'd at any rate had the excitement of the chase. 'Now, however, it's different,' he continued. 'There's a rumpus if I'm seen with a girl not belonging to the screen ... and with regard to introducing myself to strange girls ... I must step very warily.' The girl he fancied was dancing with a squat, pug-nosed American marine, but when the music stopped, she left him for a table by herself. I went over to her. She wasn't more than twenty, tall and dark, with wide set-apart eyes, and a generous, full mouth. We danced a couple of minutes and then I took her over to our table. It was the great moment of her life; and Ty fastened all his charm on her, asking all manner of intimate questions. She said her name was Estelle. She didn't much care for gold-digging, but it was so darned easy in Colon where the boys had nothing else to spend their money on except the girls. No, she didn't sleep with any of them; if she were caught doing so she would be shipped straightaway back to New York. Work never ended before six or seven in the morning; and sometimes she made as much as £5 in a night.

Ty danced with her for a while, then suggested that the four of us, I and my girl, a little redhead with green eyes, should go back to his suite at the hotel. This we did. We opened a bottle of whisky and turned on a portable gramophone. We'd been there perhaps a quarter of an hour when there was a knock at the door. Ty opened it, and there in the doorway was the hotel clerk. He was a young, freshfaced—American. 'Very sorry, Mr Power,' he said firmly, 'it's against the regulations to have ladies upstairs.' We looked at each other foolishly, feeling like schoolboys caught at a dormitory feast. 'But it is all very harmless,' said Ty. 'Maybe,' replied the clerk, 'nevertheless, the ladies must go.' And off they went. I accompanied them down to the hall where Ty said he would escort them home. And the last I saw of him was in the back of a taxi with an arm round each. He flew to Ecuador a few hours later that morning.

4

On the fourth day of my stay, as arranged, I went back to the Messageries Maritimes to see the little man with the head too big for him. He had excellent news. The *Vile d'Amiens* would dock at three the following afternoon and he'd arranged by cable that I should go steerage. I was jubilant. The ticket, for the fifteen days' journey to Papeéte, port of Tahiti, was only £8, though I had to make a deposit of £30 to ensure I wouldn't become a penniless beachcomber on the hands of the French Government. I could have avoided doing this if I'd taken a return ticket, but it was unlikely I would return. From Tahiti, it was my idea to go to New Zealand and Australia.

CHAPTER SIX

HOOLIGAN CARGO

The 'Ville d'Amiens' wasn't beautiful. Her lines were blunt and solid, and her colour a dark red. She had a single funnel, a white superstructure amidships, and a smaller one astern; the paint on her was worn and patchy, as if she'd faced many a gale since her last refitting. And even from where I stood, in the shade of a warehouse waiting to go aboard, I could see her decks were dark with coal dust. Hunched over the railings of the lower deck were ebony-black Senegalese sailors in blue overalls, and above them on the top deck passengers were queuing up to come ashore, officers in white drill suits standing at the head of the gangway. I was wondering whereabouts might be my quarters when from behind me a reedy American voice, like a thirteen-year-old soprano's half-way to breaking, piped: 'Say, have you got a cabin aboard that ship?' It was a tall, broad-shouldered young man of about twenty speaking. He wore no hat, his brown hair was brushed in waves like an advertisement for brilliantine. His eyes were brown, and his nose flat like a pugilist's. He wore a white shirt, a green tie, and a double-breasted blue suit that fitted his well-proportioned figure like an under-sized glove. 'Say,' he piped again, 'they won't let me and my friend get on that boat. Dammit hell, we just sure must go ... hide us in your cabin and we'll make it worth while.' His friend was elderly, with a red nose like W. C. Fields, and gold-rimmed spectacles. He was small, with thinning grey hair and a voice like the baa of a sheep. 'Sure,' he bleated, 'we must get on that

101

boat . . . we've got friends expecting us in Tahiti . . . Dickie Blandy, do you know him?' I told him I didn't know him, nor had I a cabin to hide them in; in any case I wouldn't have helped them, I'd taken an instant dislike to the thrusting egotism of the young man.

I saw then that people were mounting the gangway, so I heaved my suitcases towards it and climbed aboard. An Arab boy came forward to help me, leading me to the steerage along the deck, engrained with soot, until we reached a hatch from which into the gloom below was an iron ladder. I climbed down feet first, finding myself in a messroom, the size of a dining-room in a Kensington house, with two long wooden tables in the centre. At one end, through iron railings, I could see the hold. A car was at one corner and a heap of sacks and a thick coil of rope in the middle. On the other sides of the room, in four compartments, were the bunks, ten of them in each and they were fixed in couples, one on top of each other, with a framework of iron rods like the pieces of a meccano set. On each bunk was a straw palliasse and a rug.

Three men were already in my compartment. Two were tough-looking American college boys who introduced themselves as Ken and Jo; the third was in the fifties with black eyes that peered through rimless spectacles. He told me to call him Doc. At first sight they seemed pleasant enough; and

I accepted their offer to return ashore with them for the remaining hours before we sailed. We drank a lot in that time and, when in the evening we got back to the ship, the three of them were pretty drunk and, falling into their bunks, they quickly fell asleep. I wasn't as drunk as they, and I lay awake listening to the clatter of the coaling crane, sweating in the hot, clammy heat. Once I slept, dreaming vividly that I was eating cotton wool and being throttled by it; when I awoke I found my mouth was full of the coal dust that was pouring through the porthole.

I went a stroll on deck after that. It was about two in the morning and still four hours before we sailed. Leaning over the side, watching the coaling, was a little man, dark like a Greek, in a navy-blue shirt, shorts and sandals. 'Hot, isn't it?' I said. 'Yep,' he answered abruptly in a voice of the quality of Charlie McCarthy's. I leant over the rail beside him. I wanted conversation to while away the hours. 'Do you know Tahiti?' I asked. 'Very well,' he answered, as abruptly as before. 'I commute regularly between New York and the Austral Islands. I'm writing a book comparing the Australs with Manhattan.' I was thinking he was going to be interesting, when he said aggressively: 'You're English, aren't you? ... well, did you notice the anti-English sentiment that is sweeping America?' I took the hint and left him. I climbed the ladder to the upper deck.

It was deserted save for a couple in deck-chairs; the man in red-striped pyjamas, the woman in a night-dress and a pink dressing-gown. I strolled by them, repeating: 'Hot, isn't it?' They agreed. They were as distressed as I was with the night. They were in the second class and had started at Marseilles; the woman, fair-haired and slim, sharing a cabin with five Frenchwomen, and her husband, a cabin with five men. The food was shocking, twenty people had been treated for food poisoning. They had a house near Bedford where they took PGs in the summer, spending the winter abroad. 'Have you got a card?' asked the wife; and when I said I didn't carry them about at that hour of the night, she brought out hers: Mrs John Tilcote. 'I have a pencil and paper here,' she said. 'Do let us have your name and where we can get hold of you. It would be such fun if you could visit us next summer.' It was odd to meet such county formality on a tropical night.

The hours dragged through. Dawn silhouetted the Cordillera Mountains in jagged blackness. The coaling cranes ceased their clatter. Six o'clock came. *Matelots* stood by the ropes lashed to the quay. Orders rang out. Passengers in dressing-gowns hung over the rails. In five minutes we'd be off. I went below to get my camera, feet first down the ladder. As I reached the bottom, I heard: 'Heh!' whispered urgently in a hiss. I couldn't see

104

where it came from. The room was dark like a cellar. 'Heh ... you!' I looked through the iron railings into the hold. The sacks and the rope were still in the middle, so was the car at the side. Nobody seemed to be there. 'For God's sake get us some water!' Still a whisper, but I saw now where it came from. It was the young man of the warehouse, his head peering out of the side window of the car. 'We're being cooked alive ... but we're aboard!' I dipped a glass in a bucket of water that was standing on the table and took it over to him, handing it through the railings.

2

They were discovered, about two hours later, by an Arab boy. They were taken before the captain who, with a kindness which he must have afterwards regretted, allowed them to stay. I certainly had plenty of time to regret it. The young man typified the popular conception of American youth; rowdy, forceful, insensitive, vulgar. I called him Young America. He revelled in practical jokes. One morning, for instance, he woke me up by setting fire to my hair accompanied by his usual shouts of 'Get up ... get up!' and the slapping of my bottom. He had a never-ending supply of bawdy jokes, and for every piece of food we ate or anything we drank he had a filthy equivalent. Ken and Jo would have been quiet without him, but urged on by his example they were as rowdy as he was. They strutted shirtless about the decks, slapping people on the back and then wondering why they didn't laugh. America and everything in it was, of course, God's own, and an Englishman, in their opinion, had to live there for awhile if he was to become a normal being. 'Look at you,' Ken said flatteringly one day, 'you're as different to the average Englishman as a polo pony from a mule.' Though I was 'different,' I still had a bad time of it. They lost no opportunity at nagging at everything English; and they found a ready ally in Doc. He'd been a dentist, though it wasn't till he was forty that he had qualified to be one; previous to that he'd worked in a telephone company. His first practice was one previously owned by a man very like himself. 'In fact,' he said, 'I chose it because of this, so that most of my patients never would notice the difference.' After a while he decided he wasn't making enough money, so he overlooked the traditions of his profession and began advertising. He organized his skill on a mass production basis, specializing in extractions and false teeth, and ordering the teeth by the hundred from a factory. In his surgery he had three chairs and two nurses. 'Each chair always had a patient,' he explained, 'and after dealing with one chair I would move to the next. The nurse would meanwhile amuse the patient I'd just left until I was ready to return.' In ten years he worked up a practice of 10,000 patients, and then, just as suddenly as he became a dentist, he stopped being one. According to his story, as a sort of retribution for his unethical ways, he gave his practice away to an orthodox dentist who had been one of his rivals. And having settled his affairs he had set out for Tahiti where he planned to spend the rest of his life. He had little to say in favour of England. 'I hate all Englishmen for the way they fed us during the war,' he said; 'when we reached Liverpool they appeared to resent us ... we who had come to save them!' Another time he jeered at England for her respect for tradition. 'That's why you're a decaying nation ... that silly respect for tradition,' he argued. 'What's the use of England as a nation? Why not give it up to the European wolves and move yourselves to Canada? You stick to it for the sake of a lot of silly old monuments and historical ghosts.' I answered: 'Hell only knows what you Americans will do when you've got a thousand years of tradition to respect. You've only a hundred and fifty as yet, but already you respect with public holidays—Lincoln's Birthday, Washington's Birthday, Decoration Day, Independence Day and Thanksgiving Day.'

A motley crowd was aboard. Most were French officials and their families on their way to New Caledonia; and there was a score or more of Jewish refugees going to Australia.

Among the travellers to Tahiti was a barman of a Blackpool hotel who had saved £100 to spend a year in the South Seas. Another was an assistant in the dark-room of a photographer's. 'I realized one day,' he explained, 'that war might be upon us before I'd started to live ... so I chucked my job to look for adventure.' In the steerage we had a half-dozen *poilus* and two sailors; and there was a giant of a Swede who spent the days sitting on the bows, staring out to sea, talking to no one. One day I learnt from him that he was a retired postman and, on his pension, he travelled the world. On the sea he went steerage and found it very comfortable; and on land he usually walked. It cost him, he said, about £6 a week. Steerage would have been all right if my companions had been quieter. Breakfast was at seven, lunch at ten-thirty, dinner at five-thirty. Each of us had the same tin plate for all meals; and the food was the kind one would only eat if one was really hungry. There was no bath, and the lavatory, as the drains were blocked, was an inch deep in wet. I couldn't face it; and on the first evening I decided to sneak to the one in the First Class. I waited till eleven, then tiptoed down the passage. I'd reached the door when from behind I heard: '*Qu'est-ce que vous faites?*' I swung round. There, hastening down the passage, was a steward, hawk-faced and thin-lipped, in a white cotton shirt like a Russian's. '*Allez ...*' he cried angrily, '*allez ...*'

Feeling like a little boy caught in a larder, I let go the handle and ran away.

The day we crossed the Equator it was so cold that the King Neptune ceremony had to be postponed. When it did take place, three days later, it was gloriously hot and around us was a vast circle of still blue ocean. Soft clouds were poised in the sky and flying fish skimmed the water like flat pebbles thrown on a pond. No sooner had the ceremony begun than a band of people, headed by the Americans, pounced on the King, Queen, and their courtiers, and speedily broke up the Court. One after another the courtiers were hurled into the swimming-pool. Then Young America picked up Queen Neptune (Mrs Tilcote) and dumped her in it, too. Next he turned to the King, a large Frenchman in the First Class, and with amazing ease lifted him from his throne and began to stagger towards the pool. Suddenly he slipped ... down he came with the Frenchman beneath him. There were yells and screams. Water splashed everywhere. A whistle blew. An English voice yelled: 'Who licked Napoleon?'—and then, amid the turmoil, it was found that King Neptune had broken his ankle.

The steerage was banished to the poop, Young America was summoned before the Captain, and we were further punished by being forbidden to attend the dance that was being held that night. To make up for this, as the first and second classes shuffled to the music of a gramophone, the Americans began to cheer and hoot. They gave me a rocket cheer and a train cheer and other strange cheers that are products of the baseball crowds. Then Sid and Tom, two young scientists from Chicago University, got us together and read a murder story they'd written. I was the victim and the story told how the murders were discovered. It was proved that Ken had strangled me with a lady's garter, Doc had burnt my throat away with acid, Jo had stabbed me in the heart, Young America had bashed my head in and someone else had shot me. The story doesn't sound very complimentary to me, but apparently it was. Doc said afterwards: 'Great compliment to you that they should base their story on you.' And when the evening was over, I made a speech in which I said: 'I have a great love for you all, it lies deep in my heart. And it will be with great reluctance that when we arrive at Papeéte, I'll run down the gang plank, seize the first taxi I can find and tell the driver to take me anywhere where I can be certain to be away from you!'

Later, I remember, I went to the bows and stood by the look-out man, and listened to the lazy splash of the waves and marvelled at the Southern Cross. That afternoon I'd been lying there, when between the turquoise blue of the sea and the clouds of cotton wool in the sky, I'd seen, an inch above the horizon, my first South

Sea island. Within an hour we'd passed several, flat with coconut trees silhouetted against the sky; they were the fringe of the Tuamotus, and my heart quickened, touched by the expectancy of romance.

3

On the morning of 5 December, I awoke when it was still dark. I'd had but one hour's sleep, for, until long past midnight, the Americans had been more rowdy than ever before. It was the last night aboard and it was their way of telling the world they were happy about it. But I was eager to be fresh to meet the day, and to get away from them, I lugged my mattress up on deck and lay down there. I found I needed a pillow so I went down again into the messroom to fetch one. As I came down the ladder, they saw me coming and gave me a cheer. Then with Young America leading, they dived at me, yelling: 'Let's take off his pyjamas and shove him up naked!'

I was in no mood for college humour but I thought it wiser to laugh with them and hope they wouldn't carry out their threat. When, however, they succeeded in taking them off, and started to push me up the ladder, all my patience of the past fortnight drained from me like water from sand. I've never been a boxer nor a gymnast, but that night I was empowered with the strength of a lunatic. I hit out more wildly than I've ever done before. I slithered myself free from Young America who was holding my arms, kicked him so hard that he crashed against the porthole twenty yards away, plunged with my left hand repeatedly at Ken, lunged out with my feet at the most vulnerable parts of Jo, and contacted repeatedly with a rabbit punch on Claude, Young America's elderly friend. In five minutes they were at the four corners of the room and the Blackpool barman, who'd been watching, shouted: 'Bravo England ... revenge for the 4th of July!'

As I sought the torn remnants of my pyjamas, I heard Young America whine: 'Say, we were only having fun ... damned unsporting of him to hit out like that ... bloody little Englishman!' I went back on deck, soon to be followed by the others with their mattresses. For a while they were quiet, and then they began a pillow fight which speedily developed into a general brawl. They threw a mattress on to me and jumped on it; and for all they cared, I might have been smothered or had my neck broken. They jumped up and down, up and down, with a motion which Mrs Tilcote described afterwards as being like 'oarsmen in a boat'.

When they'd tired of this game, I lay quite still, bruised and stiff, swearing I would never talk to them again as long as I lived; and feeling as if I'd been transported back across the years to the days of school 'rags'. I'd been like that for twenty minutes when I heard one of them murmur: 'Let's throw Tangye's mattress into the sea!' This was the end. I wasn't going to stick any more of it; and solely to safeguard for myself a peaceful night, I swallowed my anger and said to Ken: 'Let's shake hands, we've been pals too long for our journey to end like this.' He grinned broadly: 'Bravo,' he said, 'that's mighty fine of you, Derek. I knew you would do this. Let's shake hands!' And so, with this manifestation of the old school tie spirit, the matter was ended.

But, as I said, it was still dark when I woke up. I had a feeling of impending excitement, like the first morning of the holidays during schooldays, a kind of tightness in my head. And, as I rubbed my eyes, I suddenly saw, as if only a few yards away, a huge blackness, even blacker than the night. Slowly we were passing it, and each second more of this blackness was coming into view. I left my mattress quickly, and still feeling the cuts and bruises of a few hours before, I hurried to the messroom to collect my things. Then up I went again and ran along to the bows where only the Swede was sitting, motionless as usual. The darkness had turned into grey, and within a few minutes as I stood there, the grey into yellow, and then on the eastern horizon I saw the golden rays of the coming sun.

We were moving at half speed, cutting the water as we would have done a river with no

113

current; or as if we were sailing through a giant mill-pond. Just a cool swish. Each minute the sun was stealing closer to the horizon, and the sky, and the clouds, and the ripples on the water were softening into blues and pinks and mauves and yellows. And the land which was Tahiti was transforming from its blackness into a forest of foliage; each second I saw more of her mysterious valleys, more of her white-streaked waterfalls, more of her jagged mountain tops. I stood there in the bows after all the years of waiting for that moment, secure in the knowledge that she was not failing me, that I was experiencing an exultation of the soul that I would cherish all my life. And as I was thinking this, two things happened. First the sun peeped above the horizon and shot the sky into blazing gold; and then, as I was marvelling, a beautiful scent brushed the air, the scent of the hibiscus and the *tiare tahiti* and the luxuriant jungle of the island. I was moved as I have never been moved before. I wanted to shout and to cry and to laugh. Every emotion crowded inside me and yet struggled at the same time to escape. I stood there murmuring incoherently like a madman.

And, when the intensity of the mood had passed, I found a canoe with a white sail stilled in the water close to us, a native girdled by a red and orange *pareu* sitting motionless in the stern; then further away I saw the surf pounding on the coral, and through the haze to starboard the weird outline of Moorea. Here at last was the land of Gauguin and Rupert Brooke and Stevenson; and here within my sight were the things they loved; and here, too, was the gentleness and tranquillity that filled the dreams of those across the oceans in another world.

Soon we'd reached an opening in the reef, perhaps half a mile in width. I dared not think that we were at our journey's end, because, though I stared through my glasses, I saw only a few shacks, a church steeple, a curling blue smoke, and hazily through the morning mist, two or three masts. But our ship began to turn, edging her way through the pass, and I knew then we were there; that these few shacks, this church steeple, this curling blue smoke, these two or three masts, were Papeéte.

CHAPTER SEVEN

TAHITI MERRY-GO-ROUND

I came as an impatient tourist, fancying the soul of the South Seas would be revealed by a few days in Papeéte and a sight-seeing drive round the island; like the man who fancies the soul of great music is revealed at the first hearing. I was tied to a timetable, I had boats to catch and places still to see. I could not cast off, as I would a coat, the spirit that ruled my world, the world 'of harshness and hideous sights, and ugly people and civilization, and corruption, and bloodiness, and all evil'. I supposed, in my haste, that I merely had to put my foot to the soil of Tahiti for my South Sea dream to come true; that there around me would be gentleness and happiness and laughter; that I, too, would be poised in a frame of mind that denied the existence of time and fear and greed. And so, when instead I found the scars and blisters of white man's sins, I said angrily that Tahiti was no better than the Isle of Man, and booked my passage onward; poor fool, thinking beauty lies on the surface for all to see. For what I found was the din of dance-halls, and women who had their price, and shocking hangovers, and tin-roofed buildings, and raucous tourists. A South Sea island playing the part of a holiday town. Gossip and unrest. Motor-cars on dusty roads, and mosquitoes endlessly biting, and black sand, and smug bungalows.

Such was the beginning, and I will tell of it—and then, too, I will tell of the enchantment that was mine when I grew wise.

*　　*　　*

Pierre drove me to the hotel. Fat, jovial Pierre, who in the days to come never tired of telling me in a mixture of French, Tahitian and

English, of bedworthy *jeunes filles* who awaited my bidding. I can see him now, on that first evening, hailing me in the market-place as dusk was falling, his cap aslant on the back of his head, the beaming smile on his round brown face. '*Monsieur,*' he said, '*venez ici à huit heures. J'ai trouvé pour vous une jeune fille de seize ans ... très, très douce!*' and he made a gesture with his hand of the kind of figure I was to expect.

I wasn't there. I was standing on the quay with the little American, dark like a Greek, who was writing the book comparing Manhattan Island and the Australs. Since his first abrupt meeting with me, his manner had softened, and in the days across the Pacific he had filled many hours with his stories of the South Seas. The island where he lived was Rurutu, and he had told me of the ease and carelessness of his living; and how the simplicity of the beauty, both of the island and of the people who inhabited it, stirred his soul, so that, though he was not a religious man, he felt he was living in a spiritual world close to God. I had envied his freedom and now I was standing with him, watching his luggage being taken aboard the battered two-masted schooner in front of us. But there was no joy about the parting. Things had changed since last he'd been in the islands. Zealous officials, anxious to preserve the native culture from the increasing influx of Europeans, had banned

117

Rurutu to white folk. It had been decreed that this far-away island should remain a paradise beyond the reach of those who would try to spoil her; and so the little American had to suffer for the sins of others. Luckily for him he knew the Governor and, with special permission, he was going to stay in Rurutu for three months; but even this didn't ease his disappointment. He spoke no words, in those few minutes before he sailed, for fear he might cry like a child. I watched him clamber aboard, and as the schooner moved away, he stood in the bows, waving his hand slowly in farewell; and because the moon was full, I could see him, and the dozen natives that made up the rest of the passengers, for quite a time as the engine chugged across the lagoon past Pomare's islet to the pass. The air was soft and warm, the scent of *tiare tahiti* touched me as a girl passed with a white garland round her hair, the water lapped against the stones of the quay, and behind me, from the bars, I heard the twanging of dance music. I turned and made my way towards it.

2

Papeéte is one street and a square. There are other streets rambling towards the mountains and along the lagoon, but it is in one street that the world parades and shops and drinks, and it is in the square that it meets at dawn to gossip and to buy the food and produce for the day.

They call it a town, but to my idea it is a village. Not a lovely village. White men have done their best to poison it with corrugated iron roofs and misshapen houses. Chinamen, with their money from vanilla and copra plantations, have erected monstrous edifices with garish sheets of tin. And the natives, bowed down by this weight of ugliness, have given up the struggle; you see none of their native houses. And yet there is something stirring about Papeéte. You cannot dismiss it as ugly, as you can Margate or Salford. I was wrong to say 'it.' I should have said 'her'—she is alive; though modernity does its best to throttle her, Papeéte does not yield without a struggle. Let Robert Keable describe her, Keable the strange Church of England parson, who came to Tahiti to live and write and die there. The author of *Simon Called Peter*, and *Tahiti, Isle of Dreams*. 'She clusters on a bay at the foot of the hills with a wonderful sheet of lagoon before her,' he wrote 'and she never ceases trying to subdue those who would prostitute her. She flings creepers scarlet and purple and gold over Oregon pine and corrugated iron, and she has to do it herself for hardly a soul tries to help her. Be you so kind as but to drop a seed and forget it, she makes of it a flower. Do you build a fence, she transforms it into a hedge. And day and night no power that men have yet discovered can tame or eliminate her sunrises and sunsets.'

119

She is the gateway of escape. So many has she welcomed who have fled from the madness of another world. Some like me who came in a steamer, and others, like those of the little yachts tied to the quay, who had braved the Pacific to put paid to a dream. Some who were famous like Stevenson and Rupert Brooke and some who were unknown like the schoolmaster from Edmonton and the postmistress from Vancouver. Through the years, Papeéte has watched us come and go, taking and cherishing from each one a fragment of his soul.

The steamer with the mails from the mad world was in, so it was carnival night. From far-off districts they'd come to celebrate this link with the *popaas*' kingdom. They crowded the bars and dance floors, shuffling not to their own rhythms and melodies, but to odd versions of 'Button up your Overcoat', 'I can't help loving you Baby', and others of that vintage, twanged out by guitars and plodding drums and musicless saxophones. Because for fourteen days I'd heard no night-club noise and seen few women, I was in no mood to recoil from it. I watched the men, dark like Mexicans, in white shirts and trousers with garlands of *tiare tahiti* askew on their heads, spilling their drinks and flopping over the tables; I watched the girls, their garlands of *tiare tahiti* also askew on their heads, swaying up to me with slightly bloodshot eyes. The scene was so bewilderingly novel, so utterly different from whatever I'd known before, that it didn't prick my consciousness that it was revolting. I sat on a stool at the bar feeling the same measure of power as a sultan in his harem. These girls, drunk or otherwise, slim-legged or fat-bottomed are, I thought, awaiting my bidding. The idea was pleasing. Some were, of course, gross and ugly, but there were many others who were young and copper-coloured with bright shirts, and shorts cut to their thighs, and features that were fine with the wistful, far-away look of the Polynesian. I sat there, not wishing to make my acquaintance with any one of them, finding pleasure by postponing pleasure, and feeling in the meantime superbly free. I was musing thus when Ed came in.

'What a mess,' he grunted as he sat beside me. Ed had been on the boat and was getting married when his South Sea trip was over; he was the sort of man who would be true to the girl he left behind and I couldn't expect that he would feel as I did.

'Look at Jo and Ken over there,' he pointed to a table in the corner. They were entertaining two women each, and Ken was standing unsteadily on a chair; 'Drunken louts—and it's folk like they who have brought the natives down to this.' His arm swept the scene, his eyes scowling. Ed was telling an old story, the story of the white man who in his roaming of the seas was blind in his belief that he could do no wrong, bringing with him a doctrine to rack the

121

mind and disease to rack the body. I have no time to tell the tale of the Tahitian race. How proud and pure that once they were, with a philosophy of truth and beauty so crystal clear compared with the misguided men with prayer books in their hands who sowed the seeds of doubt and fear. For that sad story of long ago read Cecil Lewis's *The Trumpet is Mine*, most tender of Tahiti books; and marvel with him how, despite the ravages of white man's hypocrisy and pests, there lingers in the air something 'that is as potent and elusive as a dream that leaves you sad at waking. Perhaps it comes from the fulfilment of a hope deep in the human heart, the finding of a way of life the world has lost, the promise that if men so willed they might so live again.' I told Ed this, but he shrugged his shoulders angrily. He was a dreamer and his illusions were shattered. 'They're sky-high with liquor and that's that. We whites are to be blamed but if they'd had any guts they'd have beaten us at our own game.' We said no more. It was not the place nor were we in the mood to discuss the poetry of living. I was too steeped in my South Sea dream for my illusions to be disturbed by drunken natives. I longed for my wakening on the morrow so that my eyes could see and I could feel my dream being realized. I left Ed at the bar and wandered home, drunk, not with wine and spirits, but with the notion that I hung suspended on the brink of something more wonderful than I'd ever known in life.

3

I awoke with the sun blinking through a chink in the curtain on my face. I yawned and stretched out my arms. I'd gone to bed alone the night before; but my hands touched something. I jumped up with a start and looked beside me. There on the other side of the double bed lay a girl, sixteen years old perhaps, like the slim copper-coloured ones of the dance hall. Heaven knows what kind of a look I had on my face. She laughed, a childish innocent affair as if she'd been amused at the antics of a puppy. Then she lay silent, provokingly unaware of her firm young breasts and her neat shoulders and her smooth bare skin.

'*Bonjour, mademoiselle*,' I said. Then I added. 'But how the devil did you get here?'

Her explanation was difficult to understand—a rush of words, half of which were Tahitian and half were French. I gathered, however, she didn't think she'd done anything out of the ordinary. She'd seen me at the dance-hall and followed me out when I left. She watched me go into the hotel and then she went to see the manager. It was all so simple. He was as perturbed as she was that I was without company and he showed her my room. '*Tu étais seul*,' she said with a smile, '*et alors je viens!*' She followed her story with a request for breakfast and a little sheepishly I went

123

downstairs. Doubtfully I said to the clerk: 'I've got a girl upstairs...charge an extra person for the room.' The man, clean shaven and young who spoke perfect English, grinned: 'Oh no, *monsieur*, we don't do that. We do not mind our customers having visitors at night so long as they do not sing and be drunk.' I thanked him for the information and went back upstairs to Rai as she'd told me she was called. She'd put on skimpy white shorts and a bright blue shirt; she wore no shoes or sandals. 'You must walk down the street with me,' she said firmly, after she'd had her coffee and *croissants*. This, I supposed, was the price of her visit. She must show off her capture. I visioned what the street might be like, all my friends being paraded up and down like peacocks on strings. I shook my head; and after a little argument and forty francs had been exchanged and I'd promised to meet her at the Col Bleu at six, it was decided Rai should go alone. With a degree of relief I bade her goodbye, and then watched her from my verandah as she strolled, lithe as a child, towards the marketplace.

Later, at the Bourgainville, my friends had other tales to tell. Jo and Ken were as excited as schoolboys let loose in a chocolate shop. They'd got blind drunk, taken three girls by taxi to a moonlit shore and played there while the coconut trees whispered and the water lapped the sand. 'Say,' said one, 'this place sure

124

is the goods … but oh Christ, I've got a hangover!' The Blackpool barman was there, too, and his tale was that he'd been lucky enough to hitch up with the telephone girl at the hospital. 'Darned lucky,' he said, 'because she's promised to tell me of all the girls who've got VD.'

Here in the Bourgainville was the Society of the island. They'd come in by cars from Paea and Puna-auia to sip their apéritifs and to gossip. White women were few. The men were English and American, dressed in the manner of Miami and Cannes. They talked loudly of nocturnal adventures while their native girls sat silent and bored beside them. These men had the air of assurance and sophistication in matters of small value that I've never found pleasant. The type that clique around smart parties and Ritzie bars and banter patronizingly with the barman. And to a stranger they pay no attention unless it be a freak produced by one of them. I never bargained to meet their kind in Papeéte. But here they were, escaping from one holiday to another, for, as I found out later, few of them had ever done a stroke of work. One, I remember, was rocking his party into peals of laughter by the simple method of coaxing a dog to sniff the bait of biscuit in his hand, only to reward it each time with a glass of water in its face instead.

The morning left me with a nasty taste in my

mouth. I had the sense to realize that I'd better move out of Papeéte or otherwise I'd be up to no good. I foresaw myself drinking rum punches at twopence a time and being steeped every morning with remorse and a hangover. And, knowing that on occasions I am weakly partial to such a futile, senseless existence, it wouldn't have been long before I'd be wasting my time like the Bourgainville clique. Besides, even though everything was ridiculously cheap, I still hadn't the money to live such a life. I couldn't indulge in luxuries. I had to count every penny I spent. Since leaving Waterloo Station, five and a half months before, I'd paid out £306. That meant I had (including gifts and earnings), £174 and half the world still to see. I decided to try therefore to keep to within £3 a week, and, as the franc was 180 to the £1, I had a good chance of succeeding. The trouble was that I had a certain amount of capital expenditure to make. For instance, it was essential to have a bicycle. Transport in the island consists of taxis and weird trucks that career at irregular times into the distant districts. Most people depend therefore on bicycles to get about on, and so off I went to a Chinaman and bought one for £2 10s. Then, at the police station I found that if I stayed more than two months I'd have to pay a tax of £3. There, too, I was cross-examined, along with other new arrivals, and given a pass-book with the instructions that whenever

I moved from island to island I had to notify the police. An irritating restriction until I learnt that no one ever took any notice of it. I had other odds and ends to buy, like a pandanus hat and sandals, and a tropical suit, and a fountain pen, and books; so that all told I spent around £7. Quite definitely I had to find a home in the districts where I could live on bananas and fish and coconuts. The quickest way to do this was to hire a taxi to take me round the island. Ed went shares with the taxi and off we started on the road of bumps and holes with Pierre as our driver.

It was unfortunate that soon after setting out it began to rain. It rained so heavily and fiercely that it blurred our abilities to imagine what loveliness we were passing had the sun been shining. What we saw was, on the one hand coconut leaves and undergrowth the colour of a green tired by many months of a tropical sun, and on the other hand, bays of flat grey water like the Thames estuary on a dull afternoon in February. We might have forgotten the weather if, as the road wound beside the shore, the rain had been falling on beaches of white sand. We could have closed our eyes and pictured the natives and ourselves, basking in the sunshine and lazily swimming in the lagoons. But we couldn't do this because the sand was *black*. Black, like Cornish rock, looking from afar like shores of black mud; bleak, drab, and depressing. Our disappointment is hard to describe. We felt like a man who owned the Derby favourite only to have it beaten by a neck at the finish. We'd come so far, we'd built so many hopes only for them to come tumbling to the ground, as we trundled over the muddy, but bumpy road. The scene was desolate and dreary, and the rain so fierce that it began to leak through the hood; fat, chilly drops wetting our clothes. And it was these that changed our feelings from disappointment to anger. Poor Pierre, we gave him a bad time of it. We let loose on him in a silly facetious way all what we thought about his beloved island, mocking the men who had woven dreams around it, and dismissing the tales of blue lagoons and sunbaked beaches as inventions of foolish liars. Pierre pathetically answered us with murmurs of: '*Attendez pour le soleil, messieurs.*' And then he would halt his taxi and disappear into a forlorn hut, because, after all, I had hired him to find me a dwelling-place far from the noise of Papeéte. He would return with a smile on his face and the information that the native would put me up if I cared. He was puzzled and hurt when I scorned his efforts. I would go nowhere where there was black sand. '*Mais, monsieur,*' he would say, '*le sable noir est très douce.*'

To Tiarei, Mataorio and round by Taravao to Papeari, we went. None of it was beautiful to our eyes, none of it tempted me to stay. Not even at Papeari where old Mauu was whom

Cedric Belfrage told me to see and at whose hostelry Rupert Brooke lived, not even when he waddled out to greet us was I pleased. But in any case he had no room; so on we went to Paea and Punaavia. Here were the districts where the white folk lived. For mile upon mile a single line of neat bungalows lay between the beach and road. They were beautifully situated if one judged it from English south coast standards. Nothing separated them from the water save for the beach—and this was black. I don't think Ed felt so definite about this sand as I did; anyhow, he seemed quite ready to take one of these bungalows if he found one that he liked. We stopped, therefore, many times so that he could investigate the insides of those to let. They were good value. They were raised on piles above the ground so that you could crawl underneath; and the windows were large and glassless. There was a lavatory and shower-bath and a kitchen and a double bed; and for all this you only had to pay ten shillings a week. It would have been lovely if it had been down Southsea way, but they were not what I wanted in the South Seas. I had no wish to hear my neighbour's gramophone, nor to have him dropping in continuously for a drink. Ed, on the other hand, was quite pleased, especially when he discovered a bungalow with a patch of white sand as its beach. This was near Rivenac's, the most famous hostelry in the South Seas. For three guineas a week you can have a native bungalow set apart by itself and European food in the main bungalow as well. Pierre showed it to me proudly, with a smile, as if to say: 'Anyhow, now you can't grumble.' But I could. The cleanliness and efficiency of the place smacked like the journey's end of a Cook's tour. The visitors, what I saw of them, were prim, well-dressed travellers, the kind that never have the nerve to go anywhere save the most English and American hotels. If this was the *pièce de résistance* of Pierre's drive, I didn't think much of it. Nor could I be bothered to look any more. The rain was pelting down; the weather was more suited for bars and girls. And so Ed and I told Pierre to drive to Papeéte. Sorrowful he was, poor Pierre; and when we offered him a tip, he shook his head sadly: 'You were not satisfied with our island,' and, as he said that, he kept his eyes away from us as if our insults had shamed him.

4

In the next three days I did all those things I swore I wouldn't do. Every morning I had a hangover; and I even booked my passage to Auckland by the boat leaving in a fortnight's time. I was disillusioned, dejected and angry. I was angry because I'd been deceived all these years by a dream. Not only had I discovered that the scenery was bare, like opera without music, but also that the romantic, copper-coloured women were like the ladies of

130

Piccadilly, save they dealt in shillings instead of pounds. '*Je ne dors avec toi que si tu me donnes une robe.*' The 'robe' usually cost five bob at a Chinese store. Such a life I couldn't stick so I took the boat to Moorea.

Now Moorea is an island that you can see eight miles away from Papeéte, lying always shrouded in mist with her mountain-tops hiding in the clouds. I will quote from Robert Keable about her:

Shimmering in the heat of the sun lies Moorea, the Moorea which one wise man of my acquaintance refused ever to visit, for he said to tread her veritable shore would be to dispel the magic of a dream. He was right, for Moorea is one of the most perfect of all the South Sea Islands. I am myself jealous for the honour of Tahiti, which, I hold, has to offer all of Moorea and more—jealous, for so many tourists scarce get beyond Papeéte, but take the schooner to Moorea, find easy provision of all island delights, and say that Tahiti cannot equal them. But the proper function of Moorea is doubtless that of providing a lovely view for Tahiti, and all along the western coast you get a glimpse of her again and again, fantastic and mirage-like in the sunlight, unearthly in the radiance of the moon, dark, aloof and a mystery as the sun dies behind her.

It is a horrible journey in the schooner, for she is really nothing bigger than a launch; and it's jammed tight with women, babies, cows, pigs, chicken, white men and tourists. And because of the nature of the current, the crossing is invariably so rough that if you succeed in reaching the other side without being sick, you can rest assured you'll never be seasick in your life. I wasn't sick myself, but for three-quarters of the journey I shut my eyes and prayed, grey with fear that at any moment we might turn turtle as a sister launch had done but a few weeks before. But when at last we sailed into smooth water I felt as Robert Keable would have expected me to feel after spending a few days in Papeéte. I was a bum tourist; and here around me was what I didn't find in Tahiti; the deep blue lagoon of Cook's Bay, the white sand and the coconut trees, all set against a background of dense vegetation and jagged mountain peaks. It was a glorious heart-warming sight for me, and when the launch stopped its engines near into shore in Cook's Bay, and I was told that, if I jumped overboard and waded to three small bungalows lying hidden among the coconut trees, I might find myself a bed, all my first feelings of the South Seas rushed back at me and I was as excited as a child.

The man who directed me and who also accompanied me as I waded knee-deep in the lagoon, was Chateauloup, a French painter.

He was grey-haired and friendly, with a quiet polished charm; he had come, so I learnt, to the South Seas seven years before, having left his wife and most of his money in the smart places of Paris. He introduced me to Madame Hildebrand, the little Swiss woman who ran the place. She had but two rooms to let and I had one and the Frenchman the other. It was what I'd longed for; the lagoon, turquoise and still, like glass, the sand soft and white, the rustling coconut trees, some tall and some short like shrubs, and then, walling us in, the silhouette of the mountains cutting into the sky. Through that first afternoon I idled in the water and then wandered in my *pareu* along the beach, disturbing the land crabs into hopping into their holes; and sometimes I stopped—far away in many cities people scrambled in the din of their daily struggle, round and round they went spinning dizzily like a top, some piling up money, some fighting for bread, day in day out, year after year. But here was I hushed in the silence of peace and of untamed beauty.

For two days I was happy; lazily, contentedly happy. This was the kind of life I'd been looking for. I awoke at dawn and plunged into the lagoon and swam slowly into its stillness, while the coming sun bathed the water and the coconut trees and the luxuriant vegetation in a golden yellow. And then, most wonderful of all, was the silence, as if I dared to be where no human being had ever been before; and, as I turned and lay on my back, paddling with my hands to keep afloat and staring up to the misty sky, I pretended I had come to the sacred places of the gods and they were watching me, laughing at the thoughts of the tiny being from the mad world. Blue smoke curled from the midst of the coconut trees at various points of the shore; and over at Chez Hildebrand's a baby son of the house sprawled naked on the sand; and at the opening of the bay, where the lagoon went out to meet the reef, a native in his canoe was paddling with firm strokes towards me.

There came breakfast of coffee and *croissants*, and afterwards, for awhile, I watched Chateauloup trying to put the glories of the bay on canvas. 'I am not much good,' he said, 'I am an amateur. But it gives me a purpose in life...' And leaving him I found, further along the shore, two fishermen, diving goggles fixed, ready with their *patias* to swim out into the lagoon. They were at great pains to tell me what they were going to do, not one word of which I understood. But I watched them as they swam, heads submerged for as long as two minutes, and with their *patias* by some uncanny means held poised ready to strike at a fish. Both got one quickly and they held up their *patias*, laughing with joy, the fish squirming on the spikes.

So the day went through, idle in the sunshine, blissfully in peace, until the evening

134

came and Chateauloup and I, sipping our
Pernods, listened to the natives strumming a
guitar and singing in weird musical voices.
There was one song I was to hear many times,
one they loved above all to dance to, with a
wild haunting melody:

> 'Puaa horo te papio
> Ei faahoro ite vahine.
> Ei aha te vahine ruau
> Mea oromoto te araimu.'

'It's about a horse on a merry-go-round,'
explained Chateauloup, 'and of the lovers who
rode him.' How lovely it was! We sat there
clapping our hands to the beats, faster and
faster, cheering and laughing, and when it was
over we got Madame Hildebrand to fill the
players' glasses with red wine, and childishly
happy they drank our health: '*Manuia*'—
'Good luck,' they cried. Outside the moon was
full and Cook's Bay an ethereal silver. Every so
often a soft breeze brushed the coconut leaves
and rippled the water. It was called the *hupi*, so
Chateauloup told me, the night wind that
blows from the mountains. A dream had come
true. Here I would stay until I sailed for New
Zealand and, if need be, I would cancel my
passage and go by the next boat or perhaps the
next. I would cut my ties with the mad world.
Hell to the rest of the journey! This was where
lived my happiness.

5

It was in that spirit I awoke next morning. A lovely morning, the temperature of a high summer day in England; not the damp heat of the tropics, but dry and lazily warm. Chateauloup went off to paint and I basked in the sun, diving into the lagoon whenever I had the inclination. I was lying thus contentedly when around twelve o'clock I was awoken out of a doze by a screaming 'Whoopee!' I jumped up like a startled rabbit. Chateauloup wasn't the kind of man to express his joy like that. I looked around and saw no one. An idea flashed through my head. It couldn't be that . . . At that moment from out of the door of the main bungalow, hand outstretched, a grin on his face, and a: 'Say, is that so?' came Doc. Never will I forget it. My peace had, in a second, been destroyed with the same completeness as the bursting of a soap bubble. Behind him were Jo and Ken and a couple of ladies of Papeéte. I stared at them with loathing and disgust. I made no attempt to hide my feelings. In fact, I was downright rude. The memories of those dreadful days on the *Ville d'Amiens* rushed to my head. I let them have it. To Doc I said: 'You're the dullest little man I've ever met and I never want to see you again.' And to Jo and Ken I shouted: 'For Christ's sake get out of here! I come ten thousand miles to find this spot and of all the hellish things you come to spoil it.'

They enjoyed my outburst; and they proceeded to spoil my peace as thoroughly and efficiently as possible. By the time dusk fell they were so drunk that their ladies took advantage of their state to go a-wandering. One came and offered herself to me, but I declined. The other went to Chateauloup. When at last Jo and Ken began thinking of them again, they were nowhere to be found. Jo blamed the state of affairs on to me and he burst into my room, yelling: 'You're sleeping with my girl.' I wasn't, but I'm not so sure about Chateauloup, who had a twinkle in his eye when I told him the story. Both he and I decided to go. It was hopelessly impossible to adjust oneself to their horrible habits.

Chateauloup returned to Papeéte, while I got on my bicycle and set out to ride round the island.

CHAPTER EIGHT

FOLLOW THE ESCAPISTS

For the next month I wandered round Moorea and Tahiti, never settling down for more than a few days in any one place. Evidently I expected too much. Whatever lovely spot I found myself in, I quickly discovered some reason to crab it. Either the sand wasn't white enough or the lagoon not deep enough or the island road came too close to the shore. And there was always the problem of finding somewhere to stay; the owners of the *farés* which I liked the most wouldn't have me; and the hotels, well, they hadn't the atmosphere I desired.

There was one at Afareaitu, excellent of its kind, which was kept by a Swiss who a few years previously was manager of a big hotel at St Moritz. His name was known by the rich and famous; princes and film stars had been his friends; he himself was married to the daughter of the proprietor of the best-known hotel on the French Riviera. Yet all the while he was moving amongst this champagne and caviare he was dreaming of Tahiti. One day he divorced his wife and sailed for Tahiti. You should see him now. He has married the native schoolmistress of Afareaitu. He has a bar, behind which he sells the native beer to the fishermen. He has a mother-in-law dressed in a Mother Hubbard and an old straw hat, with bare brown feet. He wears sandals and a *pareu*. One of his closest friends is the local Chief. But what is so incongruous is that, when you arrive, he greets you as if you'd arrived in his St Moritz hotel. He might have been Ferraro greeting me at the Mayfair, so suave, polite, and charming was he. And at dinner-time he hovered round the table as if I were paying 10*s.* for the meal instead of 1*s.*; European food, the best I'd had for months. I'd have thought he'd want to talk a lot as he didn't see many white people, but he was silent about himself. I asked whether he wouldn't one day tire of the natives (he looked only about forty) and want to return to the glitter of his old life. He gave me a gentle smile. 'I'll never cross the ocean again. I have found peace. Here will I die.' Something in the way he said it, the finality or perhaps it was so darned sincere, made me feel sad. Heaven knows why, because he required no pity. He was a man who had moulded the pattern of life to meet his desires; perhaps it wasn't my choice of existence, nor that of most people, but he had the courage to know that it was his; and he was happy.

He had a friend called Peter the Russian. Peter didn't share the same views of South Sea life; he believed there was nowhere in the world more Utopian than Russia. Not that he had been to Russia for thirty years; but the last twelve of these he had spent on a coconut plantation in Moorea, and he hadn't found them to his liking. One evening I was sitting with him in the small bar at Afareaitu; he had red bushy eyebrows, and blue eyes that looked straight at you as he talked. This is what he said:

'It's all a joke in this goddam country— nothing is serious. Natives work when they feel like it. When they've earned money they spend it—quick. How can anyone care for the women? They sleep with anyone because

139

faithfulness isn't in the Tahitian vocabulary. They despise white men whether they're married to them or living with them. They only marry for the money, which they'll hand out to their relatives. A Tahitian marries one day and cheats on her husband the next. What's the good of that? I've tried living with dozens of them, but they drove me crazy in three days. There was one I was going to marry. She had a shot at trying to make me think she was virtuous. For instance, she wouldn't let our bodies touch when we were dancing. Nor would she let me sleep with her till the wedding bells had rung. She was eighteen and pretty, and she fooled me until one morning three weeks before the marriage date. I was staying in her father's house—he was a Frenchman, her mother Tahitian—and to get to the bathroom I had to pass through her father's room. The mother had gone off to market, so I was surprised to see a woman's body in the father's bed. I looked again and had a bigger shock. It was my fiancée. Incest didn't seem to mean anything to her. When I gave her my mind, she pouted her lips and said: "So what?" How the hell can you live in a country where the morals are like that?'

Nor did he like his manner of living; he believed it would be much cheaper and pleasanter in Russia. This despite the fact that he told me you can buy an estate of several acres in the islands for as little as £100; and that you can build a house for £10! That is what his had cost him and he had a verandah and a large room, half dining-room, half bedroom; a kitchen in an out-house, also a shower and a lavatory. The walls were of bamboo and the roof thatched with coconut leaves, or *niaus* as the natives call them. Looking after copra was his principal occupation, though he kept three cows and a dozen chickens as a sideline. He described to me how every two months he collected the ripe coconuts that had fallen to the ground; then there followed a fortnight before they were ready to be taken to the Papeéte market. This was a fortnight of praying for no rain. The coconuts were cut in halves and left to dry. And when the process was completed, the price he got was £7 a ton; and he was lucky if he had a ton to sell. Peter thought the work too hard and the reward too small. When he sells his plantation, with the money he gets he's going to buy a ticket to Vladivostok.

2

It was when I'd left Afareaitu and was bicycling on my way to Haapiti that I met Gibbins. The track wound parallel to the shore through several small villages where the inhabitants gravely wished me '*Ia ora na!*' ('Good life to you') as I passed. Children stopped their games to stare at the strange *popaa*. Dogs ran barking at the wheels.

Sometimes I'd meet, in some lonely glade, a broad-shouldered native, the colour of mahogany, splitting the coconuts that lay around him on the ground. He would stop his work, with dignity raise his pandanus-woven hat, and again I would hear the words of greeting: '*Ia ora na!*' Pigs abounded everywhere, they were not fat and waddling like their European cousins. They had legs as long as terriers and they ran as fast, hither and thither, as I approached. Land crabs skedaddled into their holes, ugly shells crackling their way under the dried coconut leaves. On my right the undergrowth climbed steeply towards the peaks that lay hidden in cloud. On my left the lagoon, cool and serene in the midday sun, dotted occasionally by the canoes of the fishermen, stretched its turquoise calm towards the reef where the waves rolled in a thin white line; and then in the distance there was the misty outline of the Presqu'Ile of Tahiti.

It was in such a place as this that Gibbins lived. I met him as he was manœuvring a cow through the gate of his plantation. And, since white men were few and far between, I got off my bicycle and introduced myself. The reception he gave me seemed to be a little chilly and, as at that moment the cow leapt back on to the track, the situation wasn't improved for me. I watched him whack it with a stick. Then: 'Get in, damn you!' He was an odd sight. He

142

wore Chinese sandals and a red *pareu* wrapped round his middle like a towel, so that from the knee downwards, and from the waist upwards, he was bare; thin, bony legs like gnarled sticks, and a chest that was weedy and yellow like Ghandi's. Seeing him therefore from a distance in his large-brimmed pandanus hat, you would not expect him to have the fierce, peppery face of a *Punch* colonel. His moustache bristled white and furious with a curl like the Kaiser's. His eyes were an icy pale blue. His voice, despite his withered body, as loud as a sergeant-major's. As I followed him to his bungalow, his manner made me feel as if he'd caught me trespassing in the garden of his Camberley villa.

Once there he became friendlier and he asked me to have a drink. I expected him to produce a bottle of whisky and a syphon. Instead he disappeared indoors and returned with two coconuts. He didn't pour the milk into glasses, but, the tops being sliced off, he picked up one and sipped it straight from the shell. It did him good because, after lighting a cherry-root pipe, he began to talk; and as I listened, because of his tone of voice and his style of manner, it seemed we might have been in a London club sipping our port, the old Colonel airing his views on the world.

'Damme, sir,' he began, 'I don't want to be bothered with strangers. They come buzzing round with their news of another world I don't want to hear of. I don't ask them questions because I don't want to know anything about them. I live in a world where a man can do what he wants without pettifogging questions being asked; while you come from a world that is Mad! Yes sir, Mad! I lived in it for fifty years, fought in two wars, and dammit, sir, I got the M.C. at Passchendaele. There's not a capital in Europe I don't know better than I know the palm of my hand. I've lived in America, Mexico, the Argentine. Call me a man of the world ... that's what I am. I belong to no nation, my brothers and sisters are French, German, Scandinavian, Chilean, they are the people of every country in the world. Some among them I hate, and some I call my friends, but never do I group them in generalization, saying: "I hate the Germans, I love the French, I hate the Russians." I look at the world in detachment, not coloured by flag-waving sentiments. And what do I see? I see in some parts they're burning wheat while a few hundred miles away they're starving. I see them throwing coffee into the sea while millions can't afford to buy it. I see great stretches of land loaded with gold and silver and coal and untold riches while the unemployed hang around the streets and their wives shiver in their rooms. I read of the proud boasts of Ministers of Labour: "The unemployed figures have dropped by fifty thousand. We have less unemployed than any other country." The people cheer. The Minister opens a bottle of champagne. But what of the fifty thousand? Their work aims not at constructing a better living either for themselves or anyone else ... but for the destruction of what little they already have. For every weekly wage of £2 a man earns he has done his bit to blast to pieces a fellow-being, to shatter a home of another who might, if the world were sane, be his comrade and friend. Do you blame me, sir, from getting away from such crass stupidity?'

He rose and flung his coconut into the lagoon. I heard it fall with a splash, followed by a shriek of laughter. Gibbins shouted something in Tahitian and I saw that he had just missed hitting a canoe in which were two girls, paddling silently and strongly close to the shore. They waved a hand and went on. 'They are the children of the old woman who does my washing,' explained Gibbins as he filled his pipe again. Then he went on:

'Look at England,' he said, 'her politicians excel in pontifical speeches condemning aggressor nations. They talk about the rights of small nations, the brutality of dictators, they ooze the god-like righteousness of the British. Damn hypocrites, sir! And the people are mad to be duped by them. Her flag flies over half the world and she expects everyone to sit back on their laurels like herself! She expects Germany and Italy and Japan to disarm while she continues leisurely to take the fruits of her aggression which she now condemns in others. She utters sweet words of building a better world, but what does she do about it? She lets Newfoundland, the Gold Coast, and thousands of square miles of her territory waste in want, and then rises up hurt and wrathful when some nation, a pauper in comparison, dares to challenge her. She's like the chairman of a large business who refuses to resign though doing no work but still drawing his salary. And the nations that challenge her are like go-ahead young business men who are certain they could do better in his place. They, too, are to be blamed. Germany wants to do in seven years what took England five hundred. They're mad to think that Hitler can do this. Italy and Japan are the same. They're in too much of a hurry. But even if one of them succeeded, the world would be no better off. There will always be rivalry and bitterness and distrust between nations. They have the tortured minds of the inhabitants of Bedlam. There is no rest, no peace. I tell you, sir, when I was part of that world I was the same. My mind was like a bit of refuse on a rubbish heap. I saw no light and I myself was confusion. But here, from this spot where we are now, I see that world as if it were a glass bowl and inside are the fishes swimming round and round, without end and without meaning.'

It was a strange hour that I had spent with

him. He had asked no questions as to who I was or as to why I was in Moorea. I had sat there while he spoke as if I'd been one of a large audience listening to a speech he was making. There was none of the intimacy that is usual when two people are alone. But as I said goodbye to him, he thawed a little. 'One day, my boy,' he said, 'you'll find what took me fifty years to find ... that solitude and beauty and the simple things of life are all that count. And you're weak and stupid if you yield to anything else.'

3

When I got back to Papeéte I stayed for a while in Fabian's Hotel overlooking the harbour. I had the corner room with the big balcony, and if ever you go to Papeéte, you should try and get this room. You sit there, on the veranda, watching the world go by beneath you, and when you see a friend you hail him and talk to him as you lean over the balcony. And then there is the view. Just below and across the road a half-dozen sailing boats are tied to the wharf. Perhaps four belong to natives of other islands who have come to Papeéte with pigs and copra to sell. But the other two boats may have sailed the Pacific to reach there. For instance, on that day that I was sitting on the verandah, one boat had come from San Francisco and the other from San Pedro. The size of rowing-boats they seemed to me, the kind that sail on Saturday afternoons in the Solent or in Falmouth harbour. And a little further across the lagoon you see Pomare's islet, where long ago the kings and queens of Tahiti spent their holidays, and which now is the location of the quarantine station. Beyond are the waves pounding on the reef, except for a small opening which is the pass, and through which you will sometimes see the proud sails of a schooner sailing. And in the evening you will be the witness of a more wonderful scene than you've ever known—the sun setting, blazing the firmament into reds and golds and purples until it slips to another world behind the silhouette of Moorea. An old schoolmaster, whose name I've forgotten, was with me on one such occasion. He had come to Tahiti a year previously after retiring from his school in Vancouver. I remember him clearly, gripping the rail of the balcony, his face alight with emotion: 'Look at it, look at it!' he cried. 'How can you fail to fall in love with it?'

I played around, in these days, with several girls, bearing in mind, nevertheless, Fabian's request to me. 'I don't object,' he said, 'to my customers bringing women into the hotel at night ... but not during the day, please.' I found that conquests weren't so easy as I'd first thought. There was one girl that I liked, called Giselle. She was slim and young, with moods that suddenly changed; one instant she was playing hide-and-seek with the excited

148

laughter of a child, and the next she was silent, staring into space as if the sorrows of the world were on her shoulders. I courted her obstinately and patiently, but she remained always provokingly unattainable. We laughed at the same things, swam and fished together. Because of her I decided to postpone my sailing to New Zealand; I had no wish to leave a romance hanging in the air. Even so I didn't make any headway, she ran always away from me when love was near. So it went on, until one day she said to me: 'I will not sleep with you, because you are soon to go away. I do not want a casual lover. I am not a cabaret girl. If you were to stay and take a house, that would be different. I would be your wife and cook and look after you.'

The girls that the tourist meets are, of course, the prostitutes. There are the others who live in the districts, who are more difficult to possess. I would put them into two classes. In the one there are the girls like Giselle who, if they like a man, will be his mistress for the months he is in Tahiti. She won't ask for money. She'll run your house and share your bed and in return you'll sometimes give her a dress or take her to the bars at night and to the cinema. She'll want to show you off, and periodically you'll have to spend a day with her family. As a companion she'll be rather like a child about the house. She'll have little to say and she'll probably bore you after a time. But she'll have a manner that is refreshing and novel; and when you leave, if you have been kind, she will be standing on the quay weeping tears of genuine sorrow; and maybe you'll feel a brute that you were part of her life for so short a while. To the other class belong, so to speak, the aristocrats of the island. Their virtue is as well guarded as a seventeen-year-old débutante. You must have serious intentions or you're not looked at. The parents of one of these, while I was there, were suing a young man for the seduction of their daughter. They told the Court that the girl was twenty and had never been kissed. To say that the whole of the island was in a furore of ribald excitement would be an understatement. The young man was looked upon as a hero.

One more thing. There is, in Tahiti, no silly prejudices of colour. Because your *vahine* is copper coloured, it won't stop you or her from being invited to the Governor's Ball. The French, thank God, respect the Tahitians as the equals of white men.

4

In ending this chapter, I'm going to present my apologies to Cecil Lewis and borrow from the pages of *The Trumpet is Mine*. It is to tell the tale of Robert Keable. He used to live in a white and spacious house overlooking Port Phaeton and the mountain peaks that rise above the Pari of the Presqu'Ile. A few hundred yards away on the other side of the road is the hostelry of Mauu; Mauu, who was Keable's close friend, and, I believe, gave him the land on which he built his house. Mauu who through the years has known and welcomed the poets and painters of Tahiti. He remembers Rupert Brooke—'*pareu* of Tahiti' they used to call him, because the *pareu* around his middle was always falling down. And out from another century he remembers Gauguin. Gauguin's widow is still alive. He offered to take me to her, but I refused him because I had heard what an American had done to her a few weeks before. He had accepted her hospitality, even stayed in her house, but went away to write an article describing her as an old woman whose work in life was the looking after of pigs. I didn't want her to feel I was looking at her as a curiosity. And, Mauu warned me, she felt humiliated. But here I am getting away from Keable. The man Hall in this story is of Nordhoff and Hall, the writers of *The Mutiny on the Bounty* and *The Hurricane*. But now read on. The year is 1923.

'The author of *Simon Called Peter*, *Numerous Treasure*, *The Isle of Dreams*, and many other books and essays,' wrote Cecil Lewis, 'had always fascinated me, for he was a dramatic example of the call of the South Seas. The son of a Church of England minister, and himself a parson, Keable had left England and his parish, feeling, like many another who has

151

taken the cloth, that although he had a lively intellectual interest in the Scriptures, he had no true vocation to be a man of God. But, with more (or possibly less) character than those who plod on, he had decided to quit. He had come to Tahiti, achieved notable success as a writer, had tried (in who knows what fit of remorse or loneliness) to return to England, but the spell of the island had been too great for him. He had returned to die in the room there opposite us, through whose open door we could see some of his library, still dusty on the shelves.

'The house had remained untenanted for a year or more until Cross, a pioneer pilot in the New Guinea goldfields, also called to the island by the mysterious spell it casts across the world, had taken the house and renovated it. He was sitting in the same room finishing his lunch, and while we waited, Hall talked of Keable.

'He had Bright's disease. His sight was gone, or almost so, and having a contract to write a book a year for a big publisher (and living by it), he was in despair. The isthmus where he lived was fifty miles from Papeéte, and even there, who could help him? It was then that Hall, with characteristic generosity, hearing of his distress, moved in (forsaking his own work) and sat, day after day, at a typewriter taking the blind man's dictation straight on to the machine. Hall told me how one morning, right in the middle of a sentence, Keable stopped suddenly: "Take that sheet out of the machine, Jimmie," he had said. "Start a fresh sheet. I am going to write a Life of Christ."

'Hall had protested he should finish the work he was engaged on, that his contracts demanded it, and so on; but Keable was determined. So they started work. In one month, without looking up a single reference, without pause or hesitation, he completed the book. Only those who have tried to write themselves will appreciate what knowledge and lucidity of mind are required to marshal facts and sequences so perfectly that they can pour out without pause or subsequent adjustment. Such things only happen as a result of a lifetime of meditation.

'Shortly after he died, making his exit after the manner of the chief character in Galsworthy's *Old English*, by drinking a whole bottle of brandy. They had dressed him in his best clothes and laid him on the sofa in his study. His native wife knelt at his head, and all around on the floor sat the neighbours, Tahitians who had known and loved him, singing their mournful songs.

'Hall was gazing through the door.

' "I can see it still, Lewis, the poor chap laid out there, and that girl, lovely she was, with her long hair falling round her feet, and her tears, and all the natives singing away. It was a funny sort of end for a Church of England parson to

153

come to, I thought; ten thousand miles from home; but he had chosen to make it so and, after all, the end doesn't much matter. The girl loved him a lot, in the way they do, you know, and after she wrote home to England to his father to tell the old man—he was over eighty—that she had a son by Keable. It was quite natural, she thought it would please him I expect; but it broke his heart. He wrote to me to ask if it was true; he couldn't believe it. What was I to tell him? How could I explain this place? We don't look on Tahitians as 'natives'; they're our friends and equals. After all, it's their island. We're only interlopers in a way, and many a decent chap has taken a native wife and been happy with her. My own wife's partly native, so I know. Yes, it was pretty difficult to tell him." '

CHAPTER NINE

A DREAM COMES TRUE

A hundred people filled the quay where the *Poti Raiatea,* on her weekly trip to 'Les Iles Sous le Vent', was loading pigs, chickens, cows, cases, and passengers. To a layman the thirty-year-old two-masted schooner appeared lopsided and, as I hauled my baggage aboard, I shuddered at the thought of what might

154

happen if we faced a heavy sea. Below decks she had twelve berths but I had been warned against them—Chinamen, I was told, invariably sat there during the twenty-four hours' journey to Raiatea, vomiting incessantly. I had reserved instead, one of four bunks that were on the open deck beside the ventilators of the engine-room; for the *Poti Raiatea*, besides her proud white sails, had an engine to chug her on her way when the wind was stilled. And that evening there was not a breath of wind to ripple the water. The air was laden with the sweet scent of the *tiare tahiti*. It did not only come from the vegetation of the island but also from the *leis* that most of us had hanging round our necks and from the garlands crowning our heads. Even the poorest natives had these *leis*, dark-skinned natives and their fat wives and little children, who were going to spend the night around me, lying on the deck packed tight like sardines. Up by the bows a score of young men were singing dreamy melodies of farewell with two of them expertly playing guitars. They were going to Tupai, a lonely island off Bora Bora, where for six months they were to work the copra plantation; and on the quay their families were standing, the women in bright dresses with scarlet hibisci behind their ears, the men silent and dignified, the children clutching their parents' hands. Dusk was darkening the shimmering lights of the dying sun. Already we

155

were late in leaving. The captain was shouting angrily. A new rudder was being fixed, it was not yet in position! The passage of time means nothing to a Tahitian and the workmen proceeded lazily, without notice, to hammer the nails and twist the screws. No sign of impatience on the part of the passengers. And the captain himself gave up his ranting and sat on a case in the hold and opened a bottle of wine. Stars began to flicker. I could scarcely see the faces of those on the quay. The moon in its first quarter rose above the mountains. Ah! the workmen had finished. They walked without haste down the gangplank ashore. Orders were given. Ropes, tying us to the quay, were untied and thrown aboard. We began to move. I had expected the engines to chug but, by some uncanny means, we moved away inch by inch with the strength of the tide. The men were singing the sighing melody of 'Hoi Mai'; and others echoed it back from the quay. How exquisite it was, transposed on the silence of the night. Fainter and fainter were the answering voices. We could see only the twinkling lights of the village. And, as I stood there watching, a native girl beside me murmured half to herself: '*Un joli départ!*'

2

I did not know that evening I would not see Tahiti again. I had planned to spend a few weeks in Raiatea and Tahaa and Bora Bora,

156

returning in time to catch the *Tolten* for Auckland; and in view of this I had booked my passage in the *Tolten*. I had decided, too, that there was no point in taking my trunk to Bora Bora, and I had with me on the Poti, only a sack containing books, a few shirts, a pair of shorts, and a medicine-chest; I also had my typewriter and my bicycle. I didn't know then that I was not to see my suits and chief belongings again till six months later I was back home in England. I had not even said a proper goodbye to my friends.

The night passed uneventfully. We rolled a bit and a lot of use was made by some, of the little grey tin cans. Babies screamed and a fat woman had hysterics; but through most of it I slept. Around one in the morning, the engines broke down, and for an hour the old boat tossed silently at the mercy of the heavy swell. An old native that looked half Chinese and who was lying within a yard of me with two small boys nestling into his either side, saw that I was awake. He grinned in a friendly way; and then, as if he were offering me a cigarette in the European manner, he held out a piece of bamboo. It was for me to eat; and not wishing to offend him I took it. For half an hour I gnawed it, as a dog gnaws a bone, with the strands sticking in my teeth as the skin of an apple sometimes does. Most unappetizing it was and, when I saw him fall asleep, I flung it far over the side.

We reached Huahine at ten in the morning. This was an island the size of the Presqu'Ile of Tahiti with rugged mountains and deep mysterious bays. No white man lives there because water is hard to get. After a couple of hours of unloading supplies, we started off for Raiatea which we could see twenty miles away. The sun was scorching and I sat in the bows with the breeze fanning me with coolness. Beside me was Leon, a pearl merchant who had left France many years ago to make his home in the South Seas. His home, where his native wife lived, was in Tahiti, but he spent several months of the year sailing from island to island. He knew the history of the people as well as the story of his own life; and, in the days that I was to spend in his company, he told me one weird tale after another. On that sunny morning I remember him telling how he had discovered the last work of Gauguin. He had himself written a life of Gauguin from the results of endless questioning of old natives in Tahiti and the Marquesas where he died. In this book he advances his own theory that Gauguin never died a natural death. He quotes the information given him by a score of natives who knew Gauguin in the Marquesas that Gauguin was murdered; murdered by a jealous official who envied his power over the natives. The merits of this story I am not qualified to discuss; but Leon told me how a few weeks after he had finished the book he was in

Papeéte market looking at a lot of junk that a native was selling on a cart. Among it he saw a small wooden statue; the native thought nothing of it and sold it to him for fifty francs. Leon took it home, quite certain that he had made a great discovery. It was the statue of a leper, superb in its workmanship. He brought in his friend Gouwe to see it, and Gouwe agreed—there could only be one man who could have created it. Leon sent it to Paris and he was to hear a few weeks later that he had sold it for a hundred thousand francs.

Now Gouwe was himself a painter, and if you go to the South Seas you will see many examples of his work; and Leon, who is a lover of art, believes that one day Gouwe will be a legendary figure like Gauguin. Twenty years ago he was a fashionable painter in Holland. He was rich and successful. He held exhibitions in London and Paris. But within himself he did not feel he was creating the art he was destined to do; and surrendering his fame he came to the South Seas. For awhile he was in Tahiti, then in the Tuomotus and the Australs, until finally he came to Raiatea which for fifteen years he has made his home. Leon pictured him as a penniless old man, too fond of the bottle, living alone in the farthest corner of the island; sensitive and cultured, wrecked with doubt whether what he did twenty years ago, when he gave up success so as to start anew, had been justified by the work he had since produced.

'You must see him,' said Leon, 'because I think you'll meet a man whom one day will be great, but who now is living in pain and squalor and obscurity.'

Utora, where we landed in Raiatea, is an ugly place of tin huts and corrugated iron roofs painted the colours of rust red and offensive greens. It is hot and dusty and smelly. Chinamen abound. Prostitutes grown old do likewise. But this unattractiveness cannot take away its lovely view across the lagoon to Tahaa and the little canoes with white sails that skim to and fro through the water. Nor can it take away the charm of little Fontana, the voluble Italian, one time chef of the Ritz Hotel, London, who greets every stranger who lands there as his lifelong friend. In all my travels, I never met anyone who had such friendliness and kindliness and goodwill as this little man; and why he settled in such an oasis of ugliness I never discovered. But there he was with his shop on the quay filled with Tahitian curios and Gouwe pictures and his smile of welcome. As luck would have it, I found Gouwe with him, on one of his rare visits from his *faré* twenty miles away in Tetooroa.

3

Gouwe greeted me courteously, but I was startled to see that he moved unsteadily as a man drunk, yet in his slow talk he gave the impression of being sober. I mean that, without the clumsy speech of a drunk, he had the actions of one. He was around six feet and looked dirty. He had a stubbly grey beard but, around his lips, it was coloured the brown of nicotine, his cigarettes consisting of drooping little things that he rolled himself. On his face there were three or four red marks like cuts, though they were not open sores but some kind of infection under the skin. Later I heard him speak much of '*mon malade*' and also of his right eye which was going blind. It suffered from a kind of paralysis and, though it wasn't painful, it would close and water when he was tired so that he had frequently to dab it with a handkerchief. That night he dined with me, talking absorbingly of Theosophy and his belief in the transmigration of souls. And at the end of it he invited me to go with him on the next day to his home.

I bought four bottles of wine, two tins of bully beef, and wrapping a few belongings in a *pareu* I set out. There are no buses or cars to take you to his *faré*. The only way is a puffing steam launch that circles the island once a week. Gouwe dozed most of the time, but he awoke to tell me about a house we passed that stood white and lonely in the mountain high above the lagoon. Strange was this story of a woman and two friends, French soldiers of the Great War who, shattered by their experiences in battle, decided to get away from it all. They had no money, but the three of them succeeded, by hoboing across America and stowing away in ships, in reaching Tahiti. The men were engineers by trade and they earned a bit in Papeéte in the electricity works. Then they came to Raiatea. They started their own electricity works and in a year or so the tin huts of Utora blazed electricity at night. The three of them now decided to build a home of their own and they chose the place where this house now stood. Every brick they put there themselves, and not content with that they built a dam and an electricity plant. And because the house was high in the mountain they built a funicular to the lagoon beneath. So here on this island, four thousand miles from any city, these three live in a house of modern marvels set in a scene of lonely beauty and tranquillity.

Gouwe's home was different. We entered a bay that dug deep into the island with dense vegetation bordering the shore and the mountain rising like a wall from the lagoon. And there in the corner of the bay, built out over the water, was the *faré* of Gouwe. From a distance it looked like one of those desolated boat-houses you find on upper reaches of small rivers; and when we got close I saw that the roof of pandanus was tumbling down and there were patches in the walls where the *burao* sticks had rotted away. There was only one room and a verandah, and ceaselessly there was the sound of water lapping underneath.

Strewn about the floor and pushed untidily against the wall were his canvases. Nothing had been cleaned for a long time. Cockroaches crawled on the wooden boards, and when I picked up a canvas a bunch of blackbeetles scurried away. That was inside; but outside there was the sweep of the bay and two small islets near the reef, and beyond, the haze of the Pacific.

His food he ate native fashion with his fingers, but in his efforts to be hospitable he produced for me forks and knives red with rust which he spent many minutes trying to clean. His food, he told me, was prepared by a native family who lived a mile away; and for that evening that I was there, a chicken was produced as a special treat. There was nowhere for me to sleep, save on the boards in his room or in a deck-chair on the verandah. He himself slept on a wooden bed without a mattress. The cockroaches put me off the boards, so I chose the deck-chair on the verandah despite the acrid smell of dried urine that came from one of its corners.

But before we slept, we talked much. When I asked him why he had come to the islands, he said slowly: '*J'aime la solitude.*' And he told me how in Holland he had achieved a reputation for painting horses. Always they were wanting a Gouwe horse and he got fed up with it. Then about his drinking. 'When I get drunk,' he said, 'I become a beast. It is horrible. I crawl about the floor, humped like a bear on my hands and knees. I have no mind. I swipe glasses and plates from off the table. I become violent.' He gets up when the dawn is still grey and works through the day till the light is gone. I said something about him being lonely. '*Non, non, monsieur*,' he said. Then he added wistfully: '*Le temps passe trop vite*.' Indeed he gave me an impression that he was aware of fighting desperately against something, death or blindness. He talked repeatedly of '*mon grand tableau*' and the exhibition he wanted soon to hold in Papeéte. 'I want to make fifteen thousand francs,' he said, 'and then go back to Holland for a while ... *c'est mieux pour mon malade*,' he added, pointing to his eye and the marks on his face. '*Mon grand tableau*' was a life-size picture of two natives, branches of bananas on their shoulders, pushing their way through the undergrowth. I know little of the merit of pictures; I have my own valuation of their emotion. And this picture of Gouwe's tremendously moved me. Half closing my eyes I saw the men in dazzling colours thrusting their way through the tropical vegetation; and I seemed also to see something of the tortured soul of Gouwe. A smaller painting I bought and it now hangs in my room; a picture of part of the shore and the lagoon near his *faré*.

He lived in squalor, yet he was gentle and kind and there was dignity about him. When I was leaving he asked me to say goodbye to the two natives who had killed the chicken specially for me. 'They are sensitive people,' he explained. And it was charming, too, when in the early morning I heard in the distance, but coming closer and closer, two children's voices, singing in the hoarse attractive way of the pure native, and Gouwe's remark: '*Voilà notre café* ... don't show yourself and they will go on singing, right into the room...'

4

I arrived back in Utora uncertain what to do next. Leon was still there and he told me that if we wanted to go to Bora Bora, which was forty miles away, we would have to hire a native fishing boat. Otherwise we would have to wait for one of the occasional visits that the *Poti Raiatea* made there. We were standing at the bar of the hotel discussing the cost of it, when up to the side of us and out of the blue stepped an American girl. An elephant could have walked in and we would not have been more surprised. She came right up and introduced herself. Lia Sanders was her name. She came from New York. She'd been in the South Seas for three months and in Raiatea a fortnight. She was a painter and she was alone. She'd heard that we were going to Bora Bora and she wanted to go shares with the boat. Leon accepted her offer before I had a chance to say a word, and off the three of us went to find the captain.

We set sail at noon next day and tied up at the wharf of Vaitapé, the main village of Bora Bora, at nine the following morning. Usually the journey by sailing boat is only five hours, but the day was windless, and when we reached the pass into the lagoon of Bora Bora around midnight, the skipper was nervous of risking the drift of the sea; so we stayed outside and slept under the stars with the deck as our bed.

The dream of many people is to sail the South Seas in their own yacht, but by doing so most of the enjoyment of travelling is missed; because you're stuck with the same company for month after month and have little chance of meeting the types that make the world interesting.

Lia Sanders had a beautiful small figure so that she wore shorts with the grace of a chorus girl. 'Perfectly sculptured,' Leon described her. That very day she said was her thirty-first birthday, though neither Leon nor I believed her; but we thought it funny that a woman should add to her age when obviously she could subtract from it without fear of contradiction. She had travelled in many parts of the world; in Afghanistan, China, Java, Europe, Finland. Wherever she went she took her paints and easel and on her return to New York she held an exhibition of what she'd done. She had a real talent for watercolours and drawings, working at a terrific speed with bold, decisive lines. She had a knowledge of many subjects and there was richness and variety in her thoughts. She had a zest and confidence in life. She never stopped asking questions, nor painting pictures, nor swimming, nor writing in her diary; and after a little while her activity jarred a little. Leon and I wanted her to relax and be peaceful for a bit. She had been married very young but was now divorced; yet she still spoke with great love of her husband. 'I have no children,' she said, '... that is the great sorrow of my life. If I'd had, they would have provided me with the fullness of life.'

It was hot that afternoon we three sailed from Utora, and we sat on deck using the sail as a shelter from the sun. Lia would sometimes perch herself on the bowsprit, looking easy to fall, and once she dived into the water and hung for a while to the rope they threw her from the stern. The crew were four natives who couldn't speak French. Soon after starting I wanted to give them a bottle of wine, but Leon said: 'If you give one now they won't stop drinking until they've finished every bottle we've got. Wait until the journey's over.' That's a trait with the natives. Supposing you produced a demijohn, they would never leave until it was dry.

We talked most about Leon, Leon and his attitude to women. He was an odd mixture of cruelty and naïvety. He said that he had never loved any woman, never had said the words: 'I

167

love you.' If his wife slept with another man he would divorce her, however slight and temporary the affair might be; but he himself could have as many affairs as he liked. This was a strange doctrine for Tahiti, because there was none who believed a native wife could remain virtuous for always, according to Western ideals. Moreover, he despised native women and admitted that he'd been a rotten husband. Yet he said that if any man made love to his wife, he would shoot him. He was a strange jumble of inconsistencies. He had told me that no woman, white or coloured, could provide companionship; yet with the naïvety of a schoolboy, he said a few hours after meeting Lia, that he had met the one exception. That was his opinion for a few days and then back he went to his old ideas.

Close to the shore of Tahaa we went, wild and beautiful, and white sand lining the edge of the lagoon and, oh, the colours! We ate pineapple and spluttered the pips of watermelon on the deck and had *pâté* with our bread and drank red wine and realized that, though we were all violent individualists, we shared sensitiveness and love of beauty, and we knew that for that day alone we were the luckiest three people in the world.

Heaped in a pathetic mass on the cabin top was the skipper's wife, who was a terrible case of *féfé*. She lay below in a fever for a long time, but when she somehow heaved herself on deck she showed the usual curiosity of the native in the lives and belongings of a *popaa*. She asked blunt questions in a simple way. She could not understand the relationship of us three. She wanted to know to which of us, Leon and me, Lia belonged. And when Leon explained that *popaa vahine* was on her own, she asked quite simply whether Leon and I were mahus (homosexuals)!

The night was too beautiful to sleep through. We lay on the deck, a million, million stars above us, and Lia pointed to the three of Orion and then I learnt where shone the little group of the Pleiades; and the moon, huge in its gentleness, shimmered the Pacific in an ethereal silver. When the dawn came, in orange and gold, it was so still that two of the crew had to heave on an oar to get us through the pass into the bay. Oh, God! how lovely it was ... the great rock of Bora Bora thrusting its silhouette into the blaze of the dawn and all around us the dreamy peace of the lagoon.

We stayed in the local hotel and were not happy. A Belgian of the Bourgainville clique was there and we quickly got tired of his company; also a fat-lipped Frenchman from whose room at night came the squeals of his *vahine* whom he was beating with a stick. The same girl in the daytime had a mad-making habit of consistently playing on the guitar at every possible moment the same bar of music. And though the food was good, the rooms

169

were stuffy and small so that one tossed and sweated as one lay abed at night. I went off round the island to find something better, but I came back without news. And I sadly believed that I'd been deceived again, and that it was the same as I'd found in the other islands—noisy people in lovely places. So I decided to go, to return to Papeéte, and I even had carried my sack to the cutter when suddenly I changed my mind. There was an island a mile across the lagoon, small, with a hump in the middle and a solitary coconut tree on the topmost point. White sand, I could see, and coconut trees bordering the water. The natives, when I questioned them about it, said it was impossible to stay there as there was no water, and the mosquitoes were terrible; besides, only one native family inhabited the island. Something within me urged me to see for myself; and I fetched Lia and Leon and the three of us borrowed a *pirogue* and across the lagoon we sailed.

5

The island of Toopua, they call it. And it is my island. Beaches of white sand and sudden bays and inlets, and deep, deep water so blue and clear that staring from a canoe into the depths you see another world of many coloured fishes swimming lazily among a forest of luxuriant vegetation and rocky mountains. There is a legend to the name. Toopua means branch of

170

the *pua* tree, and long years ago it was told that if you went to the island and found a branch and brought it back with you, you would draw the island to Bora Bora so that it joined.

When the keel of our *pirogue* grated against the beach, Hélène was sitting on the sand beneath the shade of the *burao* tree, her breast bare outside her dress, unconcernedly feeding Marceline. We were at a corner point of the island that faced north. There was a view of half a circle, beginning with the far-off reef and the open sea, and then the islet where the fishermen's nets were hanging to dry, and the blues of the lagoon with the songs of the natives as they sailed by, and the village of Vaitapé hidden in the coconut trees, and the mountain climbing the sky; and there was the white beach that fell steeply when it touched the water so that when we bathed a few steps took us out of our depth. So harsh these sentences sound; but what they try to say does not belong to words, it belongs to the symphony that is found in the silence of imagination, of a dream long longed for, and at last fulfilled.

Hélène didn't mention money when we asked whether we could stay there. She beamed a smile of welcome and said that if we went back to the hotel for our things, she would have the hut ready on our return. Dear Hélène! No trouble was ever too much for her. She was tall and young with a fine row of white teeth and silky black hair that fell in two plaits to her waistline; and though she never had seen much of the world, she had the serenity and wisdom and competence that reminded me somehow of my nurse who had been long in our family; as if evil had never knocked at her door and that goodness had been her companion from the first hour of her life. Vetea, her husband, could not speak French as she could. He was that rare specimen, a pure Tahitian. Broad-shouldered, the fine features of pure breeding, and a laugh that forced you, in its good humour, to laugh with him. And then there were the children, Albert and Marceline; no children of my acquaintance were so full of fun and jokes and games as these two. Naked they ran around, and Marceline, just one year old, as sturdy on her legs as if she were three. I loved those two.

Our hut was the bedroom of the family, and on our arrival they moved over to the other hut thirty yards away where Hélène did her cooking and they ate their food. Neither was a hut in the ordinary sense of the word. Ours had a floor of white sand and the walls were upright *burao* sticks through the chinks of which, at night, you could see the stars twinkling on the water. The roof was not tin nor made of planks, but coconut leaves matted together, or *niaus* as the natives called them. There was no door. The white sand that was our floor stretched a few yards to the lagoon. There was a mattress, the size for a double bed, and it lay propped a foot above the ground on flat wooden sticks; and, because we were three, Hélène had borrowed, from her mother-in-law, a single mattress which she put beside the double one so we could all sleep together; but, as it happened, Lia preferred sleeping alone on a rug on the shore.

Hélène cooked the food. Sometimes we had bully beef and tinned peas bought from the Chinese store at Viatapé; but mostly it was fish prepared in queer native ways; *poisson cru* was the favourite, raw *operu* fish soaked in lemon and coconut sauce. One night we sailed in Vetea's *pirogue* to the reef to catch lobsters with a big oil lamp we had. How careful we had to be or otherwise our fingers could be caught in their pincers! We envied Vetea in the quick confident way he would stoop, clutch an unsuspecting lobster, and hurl it in a bucket before the poor thing had a chance to attack him. We had a big catch to take back to Hélène. And I remember, when we were softly swishing through the water close to our corner point of the island, the moon was paling our beach and the two huts aslant to each other, and it seemed to me that I was very young again and that someone had led me to fairyland.

Leon was the first to go. He never liked the complete primitiveness of our life. We had no bath, no lavatory, and for water Vetea went over to Bora Bora for it every morning with two tin cans. Besides this, I think he carried a weight in his mind so that whatever he did, wherever he went, he never had peace for long; as if early in life he had got off on the wrong foot and he had never been able to change step. I was sorry to say goodbye to him. He had shared with me moments that would remain precious all my life.

So Lia and I were left together. And we were as different as a mouse from a horse in the way we spent the days. I would laze and bask in the sun and ramble round the island. It took about an hour to walk round, lovely white beaches and rocks to climb and always the lagoon to plunge naked into whenever I felt inclined. At one point Tabu Island is but a hundred yards away, the island that gave the name to the lovely film I'd seen a decade before. Long years ago a battle had been fought there and because many were killed the King of Bora Bora declared it 'Tabu' out of respect to the fallen. No one must live there, but when Murnau, the German who made the film, fell in love with the island, he did so despite the warnings of the natives. They nod wisely now when they talk of him; first the negative of the film was burnt, and then, a year later, he was killed in a motor accident.

And when I'd get back to our corner point, I'd find Lia feverishly active as if she were racing against time, in this place where there was no time. Even when the weather was bad

174

she would sit outside busily painting until the rain smudged her colours; and then she would come into the hut and start sketching the face of one of the natives. They were thrilled by her. They would canoe over from Viatapé and group themselves behind her, silently watching. Great was the honour when she picked one out as a model. But, if it were a girl, though she herself would sit grave and motionless, her girl friends would giggle and chatter with the nervousness of schoolgirls in the presence of a film star. And if Lia wasn't painting she would be getting Vetea to show her how to spear fish with a *patia*. Water goggles tied round her head, for an hour on end, she would be diving under the water and flinging her *patia* at fishes that darted always away. And the questions! How weary I became of her high little voice piping one query after another. If only she would have rested quiet for a while yielding serenity where serenity reigned. Virile young American womanhood. How is it that nine-tenths of them have the same characteristics? Purposeful, obstinate, bossy. There was the evening when we'd canoed over to the other side to have a meal at the hotel. The sky grew dark and threatening as we ate; and when we'd finished and were wanting to return, sudden gusts of wind bent back the stems of the coconut trees with their force. We knew it was only the beginning of a storm that would soon be with us. And I,

175

knowing that the wind would blow waves six feet high on the lagoon, was against the risk of being sunk by them. Not so Lia. She was certain she could cope with a cyclone and off she started alone. A native saw her and jumped in a canoe after her. '*Matai aita maitai*' ('Wind no good'), he shouted and succeeded in bringing her back. And there was the time she bought dress material as a present for Hélène. She didn't think of asking what colour Hélène liked. She made her own choice, saying when she brought it back: 'I couldn't stand anything else they had.'

And then she, too, was gone.

CHAPTER TEN

TOOPUA

On Saturdays I would go over to the hotel for my meals because Hélène and Vetea were Seventh Day Adventists and Saturday was their Sunday. It was empty now save for the Administrator of Les Iles Sous le Vent who was on one of his periodical visits to Bora Bora; in fact, he and I were the only white men in the island. Alain Gerbault was, however, expected and, from what I gathered from his talk, the Administrator was anxious to get away before his arrival. It was all a matter of the village green. Gerbault preferred Bora Bora above all the other islands and deemed himself the most important man who went there. And on his last visit he had taken it upon himself to order the removal of two large trees from the village green, because their absence, he considered, would provide a better football field for the natives. The Administrator was angry that he hadn't been consulted; and now had ordered twelve little trees to be planted about the village green so that football games would be a thing of the past.

Perhaps you don't remember Alain Gerbault. In France he is a figure of legend like Lawrence of Arabia. In the Great War he was one of the Allies' greatest pilots and afterwards he achieved world renown as a tennis player. Then he gave up playing tennis and started to roam the world in a tiny yacht. He was the first man to sail the Atlantic alone; and for fifteen years he has been roaming the Seven Seas, frequently reported missing, but always turning up in the end. I saw him in Papeéte, bare-footed, a *pareu* around his middle, preferring to talk to natives than to white men, loping along the front or playing billiards with the fishermen in a saloon near the harbour. There is a tale that is told of him of an occasion when he was invited to a Governor's reception. He appeared as usual, barefooted and bare-chested, and the *pareu* around his middle. Fellow-guests were horrified and watched the

Governor to see what he would do. But the poor fellow was impotent, Gerbault had hanging round his neck an Order higher than any of the Governor's. I spoke to him once or twice and left him always with a feeling I would like to know him better. Once I found him poring over a catalogue from a London yachting firm. 'I am looking to see what I shall give myself for a Christmas present,' he said in his faultless English, 'that clock with a ship's bell, or that knife with a cork which never sinks.' His home is his yacht. He never sleeps ashore. When he so wills to see another island, he weighs anchor and sails there. For money he depends on the books he writes, but he needs very little. If ever a man was free, it is he.

* * *

I, too, was free in those days, when the sun lulled the hours in tranquillity, and Marceline sneaked into my hut to pull the cloth from the table, and the coconut trees whispered to each other, and Hélène shouted that my dinner was ready, and the lagoon lapped the white beaches of my island. Minutes were not known, days not counted. I rose when the dawn filtered through the chinks of the *burao* sticks and slept when the stars filled the heavens. A sort of coma, I think it was, like the moments between a dream and the wakening; worries of yesterday didn't matter, those of tomorrow didn't exist; only the hazy, wonderful present.

Maéva was with me then. Slender, child-like Maéva with the far-away eyes. What mystery, what sorrow could lie behind them in one so young? But when she laughed and played, she had the spirit of a child that knows no trouble, the abandon of a fawn on an April morning. Out of the darkness she would come to me; the shadow of a canoe on the water, the gentle sound as it touched the beach, and there she was, a ghost of the islands, running bare-footed towards me. Slim, supple body. Soft scent of *tiare tahiti*. We would lie in the warmth of the night, and I, closing my eyes, would say a prayer to the heavens—let me be aware of each single minute, none to escape, so that whatever the years may bring I will remember.

We would be up when the Morning Star still shone in the east and the dawn was a mirror of soft yellows in the sky. She would ask me what I wanted for breakfast. Was it a red fish or a black fish or was it a white one with big blue spots? A red fish I would say, and she would take the *patia* and run naked into the lagoon. Half an hour she might be there, swimming and plunging, till the dawn had become a glorious spectacle of golden loveliness and thin wisps of smoke curled from the coconut trees of Vaitapé and the call of the *pu* echoed across the water as the Chinaman told the island he had bread to sell. Then she would reappear, triumphantly holding a red fish, and perhaps others of other colours, and wrapping her *pareu* tight around her, she would deftly clean it and light a fire and we would watch it together as it cooked. Vetea would be up by this time, ready to sail over to fetch the water; and Hélène would be busy scrubbing Albert and Marceline. Maéva would wait until I had eaten and then, with a shy kiss, she would run to her canoe. '*Ia ora na*, Derek,' she would cry, and across the lagoon she would be paddling. Perhaps half-way across she would pause. '*Ia ora na*,' she would cry again. And I would echo back the words: '*Ia ora na*, Maéva!'

I never saw where she lived, and this was strange because they usually wish to parade a *popaa* before their friends. Perhaps it was that she knew I was soon to go and that she was sensitive to the humiliation that might be hers if she were mocked for loving a *popaa* who said goodbye so quickly. Perhaps, too, this was why she came and went with the suddenness of the wind. I never knew when she would appear. In the stillness of the night or in the sunshine of the afternoon, she would come and go with the inconstancy of a dream. When first I saw her she had come over to watch Lia paint. I noticed her then because she had a wistful slender beauty that was a contrast to the usual heavy type of Bora Bora. And afterwards, when she had gone, I remember Hélène coming to me and saying, as if she were passing on a message: '*Maéva m'a dit qu'elle t'aime.*' Such was the naïve way that love was born.

She had never been to Papeéte and she talked of it as a little Cornish girl will talk of London. Papeéte for her had the glitter of Piccadilly and Shaftesbury Avenue; the cinema had the glamour of the Palace Theatre. Of the world outside, it was too big for her imagination. *'Est ce que c'est vrai,'* she asked, *'que les gens en France ont besoin d'argent?'* Sweet child of the faraway eyes! Your riches are around you. Bananas hang in clusters on the trees and fish in abundance await you in the lagoon, coconuts by the hundreds are there, ready to be turned to the score of uses you have for them. Wild pigs and chickens. Hunger you will never know. And if you need the help of man, to repair the *niaus* of your roof or to build a swift canoe, your people will be there with smiles, proud they can be of use to you.

What a long procession of the good things in life you have to teach us; who send our priests to you to spread the mess that we have made of life. What will God say on the Day of Reckoning? Who will He salute? We who hypocritically and self-consciously push forth His Gospel or you who have never known ugliness, who 'love thy neighbour' with hearts unsullied by doubt and fear and greed?

*   *   *

We would take the canoe, Maéva and I, each

181

with a paddle, and glide softly through the water, I in the centre and she in the stern to do the steering. How cunning she was in dodging the coral rocks that lay secretly a foot beneath the water close into shore; and how clever the way, with the sureness of an expert, she would find the narrow passes of the reefs that circled every islet! Hot work it was after a while and we would lift our paddles and the canoe was stilled. Now for a swim. Off would come my pandanus hat that hid my head from the glare of the sun, and my *pareu* would fall at my feet as I stood poised for a dive. Splash! Hands, head, body, feet, the water caressing me like cool silk. Down into the depths, my eyes open, smarting with salt, seeing the coral in a distorted mirror that from above was shaped so beautiful. Nothing is so pure to the senses as the naked bathe; the coolness of water on warm bare skin. I turned and twisted and kicked out with my legs. Free I was! free like the fishes that darted quick from the interloper. Free as the birds in the skies. Joy raged in my mind. I needed to shout to the heavens. Up to the surface, then. A little puffed, but enough in my lungs to yell to the gods, defiantly maybe, that here in the world they looked down upon, a soul had found Elysium.

'*Tu es fou,*' laughed Maéva. There she was, a few feet away, splashing the water with the palm of her hand. Her black hair, wet from a dive, clinging about her neck and her small sun-coloured shoulders. '*Fou* I may be,' I shouted back, 'but I'll beat you to the beach.' No answer from her then. She was off with two yards start, not the quiet crawl of the professional swimmer, but with arms working like the sails of a windmill and legs churning the water like the twin screws of a steamer. How she went so fast was a mystery. I buried my face in the water and moved my legs and arms in the way I was taught at school, automatic and easy it comes to me, but each time I turned my head for air, Maéva had gained a foot. Shorter of breath I got, rhythm was broken. Splash, splash, splash ahead of me. No use. She'd won. She was standing with her hands on her hips with the water only up to her knees and her laughter pealing across the lagoon. '*Fou j'ai dit*,' she said.

Oh lovely days! They stand with the sparkle of jewels out of the mists of time. Vanity and ambition and selfishness were not my comrades then. Mean actions, thoughtless words, were driven from the corners of my mind. I was sure of myself, I was the captain of my soul.

One afternoon we lay on the beach of Tabu. Two miles away, perhaps, we could see the pin-pointed figures of the fishermen on the reef; high above us two birds, snow white against the blue of the sky, were hovering and swooping with the grace of gulls. A whisper of a breeze rustled the coconut trees, making a sound like soft rain on leaves. Out in the lagoon a school of porpoises played lazily together, and such was the stillness that we could hear their snorts as they sniffed the air. Maéva was idly chucking shells at the canoe that lay half clear of the water, not listening, nor understanding if she had done, to my monologue in English.

'Do you know, Maéva,' I was saying as a coconut fell with a thud behind me, 'I'm going to be quite different when I go from here. I've been a person without principles who yielded to the whim of the moment and was always getting into trouble because of it. I've been ready too often to scratch the surface of life, shying away impatiently when faced by problems that, if they were to be overcome, required more than just my casual acquaintance. Momentarily, maybe, such evasion has given me ease; but it's been an ease that has as quickly died as the sparkle of champagne, making my happiness a thing of fits and spasms, neither profound nor peaceful, ready at any moment to be killed by worries so trivial that on looking back upon them I am ashamed. But I'm not going to be like that any more, Maéva. I'm going to have a set of rules which will steer my life like a rudder steers a ship across the sea. I'm going to fashion a shield of spiritual strength that will protect me from vanity and desires and meanness. I'm going to be untouched by the hurts and

184

mouthings of this wounded world I live in. I'm going to be complete in myself, wherever I go, whatever hateful circumstances I may find myself in, I'm going to have the power of a soul at rest. Like an oasis that in the dry desert is sufficient unto itself, and yet gives forth strength to those who pass its way.'

A handful of sand banged down on my tummy. '*Mamu mata nehenhe*' ('Shut up kind eyes') laughed Maéva. She was sitting with her small bare thighs on her heels, and her knees in the sand; and she was looking at me with a smile that had tenderness and mischief and pity all in one. '*Quelle bêtise tu parles!*'

I was angry when you said that, Maéva, and I gave you a little smack. That made you angry too and you pouted your lips and went off in a huff down the beach. And the day was very nearly spoilt.

But listen to me now, Maéva:

There's wisdom in women, of more than
    they have known,
And thoughts go blowing through them,
    are wiser than their own.

Nonsense you had called my words and you were right: as I knew then you were right, deep in my heart. I spoke with the foolishness of the faint-hearted who on New Year's Eve roll forth a catalogue of dreary resolutions. I was blinded by the gentle spirit of happiness in your

185

people and the wonder of the world they lived in. My soul was quietened like the stillness of a pool above a waterfall and yet glowing with an emotion as if I'd heard great music after the silliness of a dance tune. I could see with the detachment of a star looking down from the heavens, the pettiness and the conceit of man, his waste and his cruelty and his futility. I could see myself wandering aimlessly like a butterfly on the wind, fired for the moment with the ardour of youth, but heading for a destiny with no purpose, no end. In the silence of your islands I felt I could conquer myself, and march forth with power and with faith, so to find a new world.

That's what I supposed I could do, Maéva, as I listened to the sigh of the reef and watched your faraway eyes and heard the cries of sea birds and marvelled at the shadows of coral beneath the turquoise blue of lagoons.

*　　*　　*

And then, one day, reality stepped in, bleak and grim. The South Seas were not my journey's end. I'd said I'd go round the world, and I knew that if I didn't there might be a restless, thwarted feeling within me for the rest of my life. So I set about planning to return to Tahiti, where I knew a boat was sailing for Auckland in a week's time. The difficulty, however, was how to get there in time. The local policeman in Bora Bora informed me that the *Poti Raiatea* wouldn't be calling at the island for a fortnight and that I'd have to be in Utora in four days' time to catch it there if I were to have any chance of reaching Tahiti before my boat sailed. Further complications presented themselves when I learnt that the *Teriora*, the only sailing boat of the island, had gone to Moapiti, a little island thirty miles away, and that it depended on the wind whether she got back with enough hours to spare to take me to Utora.

There was, however, another possibility. Into the loveliness of the Bora Bora bay was coming the *Stella Polaris*, a super yacht which at that time of year did an annual cruise of the South Seas with a cargo of American millionaires. To the exact minute the local policeman knew when she would be sailing through the pass; the owners had notified him six months previously and they had charged him to present an exhibition of native dancing an hour after they'd dropped anchor. The time she was expected was seven o'clock on the morning of February the seventeenth.

The notion of travelling in her hardly crossed my mind. In the first place I hadn't the funds and in the second I wanted to return to Papeéte to collect my trunk and a letter of credit of £50 in the custody of the bank, which was all the money I would have till I reached New Zealand except for £2 cash. So I sat down and waited for the wind to blow the *Teriora* back from Moapiti.

Each morning I'd be up early and asking Vetea what he thought of the weather, but there was always either no wind at all or it was blowing from the wrong quarter. Three days slipped by and there was still no *Teriora*. I can't say I was very perturbed; and I meandered through the hours with the same idle irresponsibility as in the days behind me. Perhaps it was not quite the same, for my mind was working in terms of civilization again, timetables and LSD. And this made me think a great deal of my family and gave me a certain homesickness; for I knew that what had been my experience would have been loved by them and I felt there was a loss in my own enjoyment because of that. To my father, the South Seas was a lovely memory, but to my brothers, Colin especially, stuck in their offices, it was only a dream. There were moments when I would have given days of my life if they could have been at my side.

The fourth day dawned so still that not even the coconut trees rustled and the lagoon was like a pond with the water too lazy to lap the shore. By midday I knew there wasn't a chance of the *Teriora* arriving in time, and I realized that I would have to stay another six weeks in the islands till the next boat for New Zealand left Tahiti. The only alternative was the *Stella Polaris*, but I didn't see how I could do without my clothes and money and, besides, I didn't know her itinerary and where she could take me.

She arrived as punctually as the Cornish Riviera Express steams into Paddington, on 17 February at seven a.m. White with graceful lines, she sailed through the pass and into the bay and dropped anchor two hundred yards from the wharf of Vaitapé. The whole island population was awaiting her, and I was there too, the only white man, clad in my *pareu*, bare-footed and bare-chested, wearing my pandanus hat. Large motor launches were quickly lowered, loaded with passengers, and raced to where we were standing. Spruce, white-uniformed sailors made them fast and out of them jumped the millionaires; cigars, wives, cameras, daughters, horn-rimmed spectacles, green and yellow checked plus fours, chewing gum and all. They swarmed on the wharf and the village green, buzzing round the natives as if the latter were exhibits of a picture gallery. They studied the local wares on sale and offered half the price they were asked. They played ring-a-ring-a-roses round a girl in a dance skirt and gave their versions of a Tahitian dance. One wit, I remember, stood among a group of naked children, solemnly pointing to each one, saying; 'That's a boy ... that's a girl!'

But amid this tumult I found a friend, a cruise official who remembered I'd written

189

about the *Stella Polaris* a year before. I told him my tale and with bouncing American goodwill he said he would try and fix something with the Captain and the cruise manager. Ten minutes later he was back and beamed on me the news that they'd take me to Suva for £10 instead of the official rate of £30; and then from there I'd be able to get a boat to New Zealand. I was, of course, delighted and profuse in my thanks; and I hurried away to collect what baggage I had and to make my farewells. They were very incomplete. I had only an hour before boarding the *Stella Polaris*. I canoed back to my island and, with Hélène and Maéva at my side, I bundled my belongings into my kitbag. There was no time to feel sentimental. I was as unmoved as if I were going to the hotel for dinner. I wanted my toothbrush and razor blades and where was my spare typewriter ribbon? It was all so oddly matter-of-fact. I remember thinking I ought to be stifling sobs and making poignant remarks; or composing in my mind farewell lines like those of Somerset Maugham's:

The breeze was laden still with the pleasant odours of the land. Tahiti was very far away and I knew I should never see it again. A chapter of my life was closed, and I felt a little nearer to inevitable death.

But none of these things were the case. Even

when Maéva gave me two necklaces she'd made from the shells on the shore, I gave her only a light kiss; my emotions seemed unaware that at that moment I said farewell to love. And when Hélène presented me with one of the beautiful dancing dresses of the islands, my first reaction was how on earth I was going to travel with it.

I left them both there on my island, waving my hat to them as Vetea paddled me to the gangway of the *Stella*. And when the *Stella* weighed anchor and turned slowly in the bay and made for the pass, I still could see them on the beach, fluttering two white handkerchiefs; but Vetea was close to us, his canoe bobbing in the wash like a cork in a fast-running stream. Then, for the last time, above the murmur of the engines, I heard him singing out the words: '*Ia ora na!*'

Perhaps it was well I left so suddenly, and that I had no time to be stupidly sentimental. And yet I wish it had not been so. Through the years I will cherish the days I dwelt in the islands, and I feel I owed them something more than the casual wave of the hand in goodbye. It is like the lover who, after his love has gone, suffers sorrow because he knows he could have been more tender. Weeks later I got a letter from my father which he had written, unaware of my change of plans, and thinking I was leaving in the way I would have wished.

'I can't resist sending you a line on this your

very last day in Tahiti,' he wrote, 'for I know how you will be feeling. It is now about 4 a.m. with you, and you will have had your last dance, and in a few hours the farewell *tiaré* will be round your neck, and you'll be waving farewell and promising to return again. And if you are wise, you never will return again, for it will never be quite the same as on this, your first visit. Many a time when fog envelops London, you will recall memories of the waving palm trees, the sighing of the sea on the reef, the fantastic shapes of the mountains, and the merry maidens' voices. And one day you will somehow and somewhere get a whiff of the scent of the coconut mingled with that of the *tiaré*, and in a flash you will suddenly be transported in spirit back to that happy isle. The memory of it will be a blessing to you for ever.'

CHAPTER ELEVEN

PROUD TO BE BRITISH

No sooner had we cleared the pass than the cruise official and the purser came to me with faces like pall bearers at a funeral. They brought the news that, after looking up the ship's rules and regulations, they'd found they couldn't take a passenger at a reduced fare.

Something about the clearance papers; they were cleared with details of the crew from the authorities at Papeéte to those at Raratonga; and so they couldn't sign me on without risking a heavy fine. Any other way was equally impossible for reasons I couldn't understand. I couldn't see why they couldn't have found it out before we started. They were eloquent in their apologies and offered to take me to Suva for the normal price of £30. Even permitting me to do this was a special kindness on their part, they told me; an attitude which made me even more annoyed. But I also, if I wanted, could get off at Utora where the millionaires were to watch a display of 'fire-walking' for a couple of hours.

Whichever I did was considerably inconvenient. I had five shillings in my pocket (the rest of the cash had gone in paying Hélène at the rate of 1s. a day—I had also given Vetea my bicycle) and therefore, in any case, I'd have to cable home for money. If I paid the £30 and went to Suva, my budget would have a big hole in it; I'd expected it would only cost me £16 to reach New Zealand. But my budget would also be affected if I stayed on six weeks for the next boat, and my timetable too; I didn't want to be away more than a year. I couldn't decide what to do. I paced the deck and puffed furiously at cigarettes. I changed my mind a dozen times. No doubt it would be cheaper if I got off at Utora, but doing so would miss my seeing

Raratonga, Pago Pago, and Apia, places which the *Stella* was calling at *en route* for Suva. Besides, I argued, if I stayed in the boat I was sure to be specially treated and given a very good time. What finally influenced me to stay, however, was none of these things. I happened to find that there were three heiresses on board, each of whom had a face and a figure worthy for the first line of an Earl Carroll chorus.

The boat was like a superior private hotel on the Bournemouth sea front. There was no privacy. Everyone knew at what time anyone else went to bed, and there was no corner that evaded the scrutiny of each passenger who had a walk on the deck before turning in. If, during the day, you were in one person's company for an hour, you could see that in every deck-chair you were the subject of comment. The millionaires and their wives all wanted romance for themselves, but the next best thing was watching someone else, or inventing a romance about someone else. Since therefore the cruise had been in progress a month when I arrived, scandals raged like tornadoes. The heiresses were supposed to be doing all sorts of things with waiters and bandsmen; there being no young men otherwise aboard. And the more mature women had properly tied themselves up with each other's husbands. Number One romance was between a widow of seventy and a retired sugar-candy king. They'd get tipsy together each evening, take part for a while in the dancing, and then retire to a certain corner of the deck to coo under the moon, apparently unaware that the rest of the company were watching. This sugar-candy king talked to me about his love for the widow, explaining that it was a rebound. He told me that his own wife had run off with a younger man. Then added confidentially: 'She's at her change of life, you know. Perhaps when that is all over, she'll change her mind.'

I was thought to be a 'genu-ein' beachcomber, so that I came in for a full share of attention. Certainly I must have looked odd, wandering bare-footed round the deck with very little else on; while the rest wore what Fifth Avenue shops imagined were the mode in the South Seas. One millionaire after another asked me for my story and each one got it more and more embroidered. I thoroughly enjoyed myself; and I shamelessly made use of my inventiveness as a means of getting free drinks.

Attention from the cruise management was, however, not forthcoming. They allotted me a poky little inside cabin with no windows at all—this for £3 a day on a millionaire's luxury yacht! As it happened, the *Stella Polaris* was built for cruising in cold northern waters, not in the tropics; and the design of all her cabins assured their occupants the maximum of heat and the minimum of air. The millionaires were paying around £2000 for the three months' cruise, besides current expenses, which must have been colossal considering the cocktail parties they gave and the curios they bought in bulk at each port.

The cruise management must have felt I was a pauper in comparison with these lavish spenders. In fact, my first four days aboard were most embarrassing as I had no money at all, and though I knew there would be an answer to my cable in time, I could feel doubt growing each day in the minds of the management as to whether I was completely bogus or not. It was with glee that, one evening, I was able to inform them that £50 had been placed to my credit at the ship's agents. Meanwhile I had also cabled the Consul at Papeéte to forward my luggage to Sydney together with my money; even so I knew that the odds were against my ever contacting them, as I would probably have left Sydney by the time they arrived. Anyhow I paid over the £30 and, by the end of the voyage, another £5 for tips and my bar bill. I had therefore £15 when we sailed into Suva, which had to keep me there five days and also pay for my ticket to Auckland. It was so little that the Suva passport authorities wouldn't let me land until, after an hour's arguing, they produced a police sergeant who escorted me to a booking agent's where he watched me buy a third-class ticket to Auckland for £7; then they were satisfied they'd be able to turn me out of the Fiji Islands if I spent the rest of my money. As it happened, however, I was lucky; and I went away from Suva with more money than I had when I arrived; but that'll be told in a moment.

For six days of the voyage the weather was most untropical. A high wind that sent the boat lurching from side to side. And it was so bad at Raratonga that we were unable to land. There is no wharf or lagoon to shelter in there; the boat anchors a half-mile from shore and you go the rest of the way by launch. I wasn't therefore able to verify the proud boast of a New Zealander I met in Tahiti who said: 'Raratonga is a damned sight better place than this hole. The natives are taught to respect a white man there—and they damn well get off the pavement when one comes along.'

From there we went to Pago Pago (pronounced Pango Pango), which has earned renown as the spot where Somerset Maugham wrote *Rain*. It must have been on such a day as we arrived that he had his inspiration. It was like a shower-bath, turned full on. Hour after hour it fell unceasingly; and the ninth day in succession, somebody told me. The inevitable native dances were held under cover. Broader of face and body than the Tahitians the natives seemed to be. Obviously they'd taken after their American masters in a love of gold. One naked little boy, in a corner of the warehouse where the performance was taking place, did a roaring business, despite the bad light, by posing for his picture. Each time a millionaire

197

produced a camera, the little boy chirped: 'Me don't stand still till you give me dollar!'

An afternoon was our allotted time there and then we left for Apia. To the dismay of the cruise management we arrived two hours late, so our visit was cut down to three hours. Off went the millionaires to Stevenson's tomb like a pack of hounds. That was the sort of excursion they'd be able to brag about to their heart's content when they got back home; and surely this Jules Verne journey, under the wings of trained nurses, had no other purpose than to provide them with subjects to brag about? For what was left of their lives they'd be able to say unctuously to their old cronies: 'When I was in Tahiti ... when I was in Apia.' As it was, after spending a couple of hours in a South Sea island they'd say: 'What a horrible place compared with Raiatea'; and 'How unfriendly the people of Pago Pago are.' Ugh, what ants!

I spent my time in Apia talking to Olaf Nelson, a big, double-chinned half-caste with a deep musical voice who has twice been deported by the New Zealand Government (who control this part of Samoa) for his nationalistic activities among the people. Samoa used to be German and the New Zealand Government keep a watchful eye that there aren't demonstrations in favour of going back to Germany. As it happens, there's not much to fear of this because, Olaf Nelson explained to me, the average Samoan dislikes the Germans as much as he does the New Zealanders: what he wants is Samoa for the Samoans, and he includes American Samoa in that as well. When Nelson has been in trouble it's because he's been urging for wider powers to be given to the natives. In this he has succeeded in achieving a great deal, and as he said to me: 'We're quite satisfied with the Government at the moment.' What he couldn't understand, however, was why the New Zealand Government had allowed a Nazi school teacher to come to Apia to teach the children of the thirty-six Germans in the islands; especially as he flew the Nazi flag over his school. I couldn't understand myself and I had no time to find out; sitting in Olaf Nelson's office I heard the *Stella's* siren and I had to rush back.

2

And so to Suva. I stood on the quay and waved my handkerchief at the millionaires as the *Stella* moved away. I was quite sorry I'd been left behind. Some of them had been very charming, and it was going to be dull and quiet after the noise of the past ten days. I had taken a room in the cheapest hotel, and there I had to stay till the New Zealand boat left in five days' time. My first impression of Suva had not been favourable. The heat was the kind that kept one's clothing perpetually clinging to one's body; and the natives were fuzzy-wuzzies with none of the attractiveness of the Polynesians. There were many white women, but the climate gave them no help; one and all seemed to be flat-chested and their faces were tight-skinned and without colour. The men, too, looked tired, as if every movement was an effort. There was none of the irresponsibility of Tahiti. Here was a country where white men ruled and dressed for dinner and looked upon the coloured man as a servant.

It was in gloom therefore that I left the quay and wandered back to the hotel. For the life of me I couldn't see how I was going to fill in my time. I hadn't the money to go on any excursions, and so I couldn't see myself doing anything else than hanging around the hotel lounge. It was a dreary spot, with the Fijian equivalent of aspidistras and a green parrot with a persistent shrill whistle, and prints on the walls of Wellington at Waterloo and a setter carrying a pheasant. And the chairs were hard.

I got back and found a letter awaiting me. This was a surprise as I knew no one in the islands. And what I found inside made me call for a drink. Neatly folded around a card were two crisp £5 notes!

'Happy birthday and good luck,' was written on the card—and it was signed by one of the heiresses! I was thankful the *Stella* had already sailed. There could be therefore no question of my returning them: at the same time I was grateful that anyone should think of giving me such a gift and be so tactful as to hand it over after they'd gone. I wasted no time in sending an ecstatic cable to the *Stella*.

The situation was now considerably changed. I was able to buy several things that would help me to look a little more respectable when I arrived in New Zealand. I got, for instance, a white gabardine suit made for me. It cost 30*s*. at an Indian tailors. Then there were shirts, and a pair of shoes; and I was able to instruct a solicitor to draw up a power of attorney in the name of the British Consul in Tahiti, a procedure I'd learnt was necessary if the Consul was to get my money from the bank. But as the charge for this was £3, it was soon that I'd little of the £10 left. In fact, I had none to spare which might have enabled me to see more of the Fiji Islands than Suva. Despite my good fortune, I still had to loaf around the hotel.

Since I knew nothing of Fiji, I decided to fill the hours by finding out something about it. So, from the local newspaper editor, the publicity officer, and the chief of the local BBC I discovered such facts as that Indians, Fijians, and Europeans each have five representatives on the Legislative Council; that these are more an advisory body than anything else since Fiji, being a Crown Colony, is governed by benevolent despotism, e.g. the Governor. The

201

main problem, however, facing the Colony is the ever-increasing Indian population. In the 1936 census there were ninety-eight thousand Fijians and eighty-five thousand Indians, but though the birth-rate of the two races is about the same, the Fijians have a higher mortality rate. In the not too far distant future therefore there will be more Indians than Fijians; as it is, the Indians, being harder working and cleverer, have ousted the Fijians from many spheres of the economic life of the islands. What people are wondering is what is going to happen when they are no longer the minority.

Other scraps of information I collected included that about the gold mine, though only discovered in 1931, which was now producing a £1000 worth of gold a day. And that though the Berlin and Rome radio stations were easily heard, Daventry was so faint that no one could be bothered to listen to it. And that the Japanese were fortifying the Caroline Islands which were only two-days' sailing from Suva. It was here in Suva, incidentally, that I first knew people who were in real fear of the yellow terror, in much the same way as Londoners fear air raids. Fiji, so the locals thought, would provide an ideal base for the Japanese as a jumping-off ground for an attack on New Zealand. The armed forces in Fiji, so they said, were hopelessly inadequate for defending the islands and the Japanese would have no difficulty in overcoming them. As it is today, however, Japanese are forbidden to enter the islands just as they are forbidden by the French to enter the Society Islands.

After these five days in Suva, I left by the *Niagara* for Auckland. It was an uneventful journey. In a burst of extravagance, knowing that £100 was waiting for me at Auckland, I changed my third-class ticket to a first-class. It gave me a cabin to myself and an Australian steward who preferred grousing to working; so bad-tempered was he that when I asked him to press my trousers he told me to go and do it myself. He accused Australia of being riddled with graft, and the union bosses, both there and in New Zealand, to be racketeers who had no regard for the men whose welfare they were paid to look after. He said that the cost of living in Australia had risen a £1 a week in one year and that both countries were heading for bankruptcy. The rulers, he said, had no idea of ruling, yet resented advice from Englishmen and Americans who might know better. Always at the back of their minds, however, was the secure knowledge that if bankruptcy did come upon them, they would be helped out of it by loans from the old country.

3

I heard more sentiments like these when I reached Auckland. From the first small shopkeeper I met, a tailor who sold me a tie in his shop a few hundred yards from the quay, I

203

heard these words: 'We are too young to govern ourselves. We want a Colonial Government.' He surprised me. I fully expected a somewhat arrogant 'we can manage better without you' sort of attitude, both on the part of New Zealanders and Australians. But what this man said was typical of what I later heard from small wage-earners of both countries; though I don't mean to be misleading by coupling New Zealand and Australia together. Each has her own problems and each is profoundly jealous of the other; it is only their common attitude to the Mother Country which I found the same and which surprised me.

The tailor went on to talk to me about wages. Wages have risen with a jump since the Labour Government came into power. Laws have been passed making union membership compulsory for those over eighteen; and a sliding scale of wages has been introduced into every trade and business of the country. A male clerk of twenty-three, for instance, now gets £4 sterling a week compared with 45s. in 1936. The same for a shop assistant. Eight hours is a working day, and overtime is paid at time and a half for the first four hours and double time afterwards. Road labourers get £3 10s. sterling for a forty-hour week. A farm labourer gets £4. Maidservants get 26s., with board, for a forty-eight-hour week. Warehouse workers used to get 45s. and now get £4 a week. As far as waterside workers are concerned, no one knows what they earn. They are scheduled to have 2s. 8d. an hour for a forty-hour week. Then there is the overtime which they arrange for themselves day after day. My tailor friend told me that he numbered several, among his acquaintances, who were collecting £20 every Friday, who were running cars and renting houses in the residential area of Auckland.

'Everyone is in favour of higher wages,' he said, 'so long as there is plenty of money to pay them; but many of us who have even benefited are now wondering how long it will last. The Government have placed so many restrictions on business, profits have so fallen, and the cost of living so increased, that we can't help thinking that these fine days may end in bankruptcy.'

There is no doubt what the business leaders think. Those whom I saw were filled with gloom—like those the world over when profits are not effortlessly filling their pockets. They admitted that the idea of the Government to make the country self-supporting was admirable in theory, but they were quite certain it couldn't work out in practice. The chief reason was the small population of New Zealand, which is only one million four hundred thousand. No firm could therefore build a factory and make it pay. For instance, an electric light bulb factory, with only thirty employees, would supply the needs of the whole country in six months. A steel factory, with a minimum organization of staff, would produce enough steel in three months. A motor-car factory would turn out enough cars in four months. And so on. Besides this lack of a market, the factories are faced with exceptional overheads owing to the high level of wages.

Then the business men have hard things to say of the Government's control of their money. The banks are controlled by the Government and not a penny of a private person's money is spent without them knowing it. They allege that it is as hard to get a New Zealand pound out of the country as it is to get ten marks out of Germany. In this respect I can support them. My £100 sterling was waiting for me when I arrived, but when I informed the bank manager that I was taking all but a few pounds of it to Australia, he explained that I would have to fill up various forms and receive the permission of the Government before I could do so. I got the permission after eight days, but I was luckier than some other tourists. An Englishman from India had £300 left after spending six months in the country, but when he applied to take it home with him, he was informed he couldn't take more than £20. And there was a London woman who was refused permission to take £500 of her money back to England.

I was lucky to have my uncle living near

Auckland and it was thanks chiefly to him that I learnt so much in so short a time; and my own sketchy opinion of the situation was that it wasn't as bad as people made out. Certain aspects such as those I've just mentioned I didn't like. Also the fact that if a newspaper attacks the Government, the unions call a strike in the paper concerned; that sounds too much like the other end of a dictatorship. The Government, however, have had the courage to try something new, to make a gigantic experiment. Its supporters admit that adjustments will have to be made, but they're confident that a balance will be secured in time. Then, they say, New Zealand will be the envy of the world because her people will have a higher standard of living than any other nation. If, on the other hand, the experiment fails, because of the war or for some other reason, they do not feel they will suffer, because, as a union secretary put it to me: 'We know that Britain will not let us sink into inflation and bankruptcy.'

4

This reliance on Britain I found in Australia as well. It was the confidence of a rich man's son who knows that if he gets into trouble, his father will help him out; not that he intends to ask for help unless he absolutely needs it; only, unlike an orphan or a poor man's son, he has a background behind him in which he can shelter if it comes to the worst. Neither Australia nor New Zealand have any intention to shirk their end of the partnership. That's old news, the war has proved that. But when I arrived in Sydney, since it had so often been drilled into me that the Empire was breaking up, I believed it to be true; and on every side of me I expected to hear words of determination to steer clear of European entanglements at all costs; and if Britain got mixed up in a war, well, that was just too bad. Within five minutes of my landing, however, on that sunny morning when the world's newspapers were screaming Hitler's march into Prague, the driver of the taxi which was speeding me to my hotel shouted over his shoulder: 'We have to slam that man from the face of the earth some time or other, so why don't we get on with it now?' I was to hear plenty more of that kind of talk, from labourers, business men, shop assistants, railway porters; and it was always the word 'we' that they used, never 'you'.

Strangely enough they weren't at all impressed at the appointment of the Duke of Kent as Governor-General. I found them hypersensitive as to what the old country thought of Australia, and they imagined they could see in this appointment a double meaning; as if Britain doubted the loyalty of Australia and was sending a Royal Duke to win her over. They argued they couldn't be any more loyal than they already were and Royalty in the country could only result in snobbishness among the wealthy; while the poor would look upon it as a waste of time and expense. As for myself, I'd hoped to make some money out of the Duke of Kent; and that there would be one or two letters from London commissioning me to write articles on his home, etc. I was, however, needlessly optimistic. There wasn't a line.

Sydney was so hot that you could have fried eggs and bacon on the pavement any hour of the day. Thinking that by having a smart address I'd be more likely to impress the local newspapers, I took a poky little room on the top floor of the Australia Hotel. Again I was out of luck. I was quite unable to bluff them into hiring me to do anything. They proffered the old story of being willing to read anything I cared to submit, but this I was too lazy to do; firstly because I couldn't risk the inevitable expense which I'd have to pay out when collecting material, and secondly, even if an article was accepted, payment was very small. I had worked out that I could spend £20 in Australia and not a penny more. That would leave me with £25 for the fare to Japan, £40 for the fare across Siberia to England and a measely £10 to spend on the way. I had, however, yet to find out whether I could get a visa for Japan and another visa to take me through Russia. Many people had warned me that, since I was described on my passport as a journalist, neither Japan nor Russia would want me. I was, therefore, fully prepared to find I'd have to go home by another way; and I'd already made up my mind that this would be via America. Luckily, on my first evening in Sydney I met the Japanese Consul-General at a party and he assured me that he would be only too pleased to give me a visa. 'The more Englishmen to see my country, the better,' he said. But whether I got a Russian visa would have to remain in doubt until I saw the Soviet Embassy in Tokyo.

I therefore booked a second-class ticket on the *Kamo Maru*, leaving Sydney on 2 April. The price of £25 was reasonable since it was a five weeks' voyage, and the boat was calling at Brisbane, Thursday Island, Davao, Manila, Hong Kong, Shanghai and five ports in Japan before reaching Yokohama; I could, however, if I wished, either break my journey at any port on the way or get off at Kobe and have a free train fare to Tokyo. How I was going to live within my £10 pocket money I refused to think; but I had a feeling that somehow it would be all right.

Meanwhile, in addition to my Suva gabardine suit, I'd bought a pair of grey flannel trousers and a double-breasted blue flannel coat. These I wore every day (and continued to do so till I reached home two months later) since gabardine suits seemed to be out of fashion in Australia. On occasions, unfortunately, I was invited to parties where evening dress was worn; and then I appeared in my white gabardine trousers, my double-breasted blue coat, a white shirt and a black bow tie.

On the first occasion I arrayed myself like this, I'd been invited out to dinner at Princes. This is a dance restaurant equal in its band, its food and the glamorous women numbered among its customers, to any top flight restaurant in London or New York. I confess I had come to Australia in the same condescending mood as a Londoner goes to Manchester. I expected the women to have bad skins, dowdy clothes and voices you could cut with a saw; and the men to be bronzed Tarzans who, in scanty shorts, lounged the day through on the beaches. Quite wrong of course I was. At Princes that evening one girl after another had a figure and looks of a film star; and wore her clothes with the chic and poise of a young American rather than the gaucheness of an English débutante. The men, too, were like any of the young men about town seen around Fifth Avenue and Mayfair; and yet a dozen I met of both sexes had their homes hundreds of miles away in the bush and a visit to Sydney was as much an adventure as a Londoner's visit to Paris. Later in Melbourne it was the same. And in both cities, except in Hollywood, I had never seen such a universal slimness of figure and prettiness of face among typists, shop assistants, waitresses and usherettes. Their knowledge of clothes and make-up leave the English far behind.

Yet you quickly sense the inferiority complex they have of English people. The whole nation suffers from it and the mirror of the affliction is in the newspapers. They are like English provincial newspapers except they are four thousand miles away from London instead of a hundred or so. All the page lead stories are London stories; and, like as not, any story on Australia is dated from London. In the gossip columns London is always being mentioned, either concerning someone who is going to London or someone who has come from London. People talk about a trip to London in the same way as a film-struck girl talks of a trip to Hollywood. Those who have done it can dine out on their experiences for years to come and affect a snobbishness when the name of a famous politician crops up, like the schoolboy who knows the captain of the school cricket eleven in the holidays; even though they've never even seen the man. And, of course, the most popular sales talk of a shop assistant is to say that the article is the latest thing in London.

5

For ten days in Sydney I kept to the minimum expense while at the same time appearing as comfortably off as possible. The pretence was beginning to bore, but for good or for evil I imagined I'd more chance making money by looking prosperous than by looking down and out. At a cocktail party I met an English theatrical producer who at one time in London was as well known as C. B. Cochran. He buttonholed me in a corner and expounded a grandiose scheme to bring out world-famous actors and actresses to Australia over a period of two years, thus coinciding with the stay of the Kents. He explained that he had already £20,000 as backing, and that his next step was to persuade such people as Noel Coward, the Lunts, and Charles Laughton, that it was worth their while to spend three months touring Australia. In this he thought I could help by writing an article on the theatrical possibilities of the southern hemisphere; and so that he might explain his plans more fully, he invited me to lunch at Princes the following day.

As we sat down at a sofa table and we were looking at the menu, I heard him say: 'The lunch is on you.' He said it in the tone of voice as one says: 'The lunch is on me.' And so the words didn't sink into me and instead I replied: 'Oh no, don't be silly ... let's each pay for our own.' This offer I made in half-hearted politeness, hoping he wouldn't accept it as I'd spent my quota for the week and I would have had a sandwich lunch if he hadn't asked me to Princes. After we'd ordered the food, he said:

'What would you like to drink?' I looked at the wine list and with his help chose a Liebfraumilch. It was very good and expensive; and as we sipped it and ate the excellent food, he told me of his past successes and failures in London. How he had lost £300,000 two years previously but how he had since redeemed his losses in Australia. If only he could succeed in signing a half-dozen big names for an Australian tour, he would make so much money that he would return to London and put on bigger shows than ever. He talked with a kind of boyish enthusiasm that was charming; and what with the wine and the good food, by the time the coffee came I was beginning to like him. At that point he asked the waiter for cigars and two Biscuit Débouche's 1889; before they arrived however I offered him a Player's. He looked at it and said: 'Oh, I must smoke Craven A,' and he called the cigarette girl for a packet, telling her to put it on the bill. For three-quarters of an hour more we were together as he told tales of his exploits in the theatrical world, and then he called for the bill. Without a flicker of an eyelid he took a glance at it and pushed the plate over to me. It was done with such an air of confidence that I lost my senses. Without a murmur I brought forth my notecase and paid for it. He continued talking to me as if nothing unusual had happened and didn't stop until we'd walked up the stairs to the street. Then he paused, and looking at me said: 'I'm going to make an extraordinary request ... I'm going to see my lawyer at six-thirty ... but until then I've only fourpence ... could you, old man, lend me £1?' That was the last straw. Feebly I said I hadn't a £1 but would two bob do? Apparently it would, because with a gay: 'Thanks, old man,' he pocketed the coin and went off.

The next day I went off to Melbourne for the weekend. I arrived in time to get to the opening night of the Russian Ballet and to see Baronova, Gregoroeva and Anton Dolin among others, dancing to an orchestra which was too small to drown the squeaks of the floorboards. Afterwards I was taken to a party for the performers, and when Sevastianov, Baronova's husband, heard that I might be going to Moscow, he asked me to give a message to his sister who is an actress there. Most interesting person present however was Stuart Menzies, now Prime Minister of Australia, but then in the wilderness after resigning from the Attorney-Generalship. In actual fact, ten days after my seeing him, Lyons the Premier died; and a few days after that Menzies had taken his place. Amid the chirrup of ballet talk, he told me that it was his conviction there would be no war for two years. But if there was, we need have no fear of the Empire not standing together. He assured me that both Australia and Canada would be even more warlike than the English. 'There is a deep conviction in every Australian's heart that once we take the lone road, we are lost.' He is a big man, over six foot in height; though his hair is thin and white, his face does not look old. He has a deep voice with only a slight Australian accent. He has a way of fixing his whole attention on you when he is talking or when you are talking to him. He is surprising both critics and friends by the way he is holding his office. Most people thought he was the one man in Australia for the job but few thought he was strong enough to keep the members of his Government in harmony for long.

From Melbourne I went to Canberra. It was a night train, and at Goulburn at eleven o'clock I had to change to the small branch line that runs to the capital. Just as the train was about to pull out a man tumbled into my compartment, his necktie askew and his face perspiring. 'Heaven knows what the reporters will say after that!' he gasped. I looked intelligent, pretending I knew exactly who he was, and asked: 'Were they unpleasant?' He smiled, a nice smile of a man who had seen a lot of life and who had always kept his sense of humour. He looked about forty, a lean bronzed face which made his eyes startlingly blue. He reminded me at once of Lord Nuffield. 'Oh no. They were all right,' he answered.

For twenty minutes we talked on various

topics of the day. He appeared as interested to hear what I had to say as he was to talk himself. I tried hard to discover from his remarks who he might be but without result; until at last I said to him: 'I suppose this scare talk of war on the part of the Government is just the old dodge of taking the people's mind off the social problems of the country?' There was a pause. He coughed. 'Oh no, it isn't,' he said, 'and I happen to know. You see, I am Minister of Defence!'

His name was Brigadier Street. More than anyone it is he that should have the kudos for the state of preparedness on the part of Australia. In a quieter way than Hore-Belisha he effected a number of reforms in the Australian army over the past three years. I asked him whether he thought Japan to be threatening Australia. 'Not yet,' he said, 'their hands are full for some years to come. But we must never forget that Darwin is nearer their Caroline Islands than it is to Sydney.' He is dead now, killed in an aeroplane accident; but not before he had laid the foundations of Australia's great war effort.

I spent two days in Canberra. I went over 'Yarrumla,' the residence of the Governor-General where the Kents were to live, a lonely, uncomfortable house which the Government were making great efforts to improve; in fact they'd budgeted £20,000 to be spent on it. And for the rest of the time I meandered about the spacious avenues and parks. It is more like a health spa than a capital. No houses line the roads except the few official residences of those connected with the Government. The station with its wooden fence reminded me of Bodmin Road in Cornwall.

In Canberra at the time was the British Air Mission, one of whose members was Sir Donald Banks who had already achieved remarkable results in the organization of aeroplane factories in Canada. I'd met him once in London with my brother Nigel, and as he was on the same train going back to Sydney I sat with him for a while. Most of what he said I have forgotten, but there was one sentence which he said so decisively that I noted it down. 'We have two wars to fight,' he said, 'first we must beat Germany ... and then Russia.' He spoke with the same matter-of-fact conviction as one talks of winter following autumn. It chilled me with fear, the first time for many months that reality of the sores in the world were once more in my mind. I remember when late that night I reached my hotel I left my bags and then went out again to walk along the deserted streets. The world was caught in a trap from which there was no escape. It was no use deceiving oneself. If not this year, then the next. Perhaps it would have started even before I got back. And for a fleeting moment I thought of cancelling my passage to Japan and taking the first boat home.

218

CHAPTER TWELVE

WHO LIKES THE JAPANESE?

I went aboard the *Kamo Maru* with only the barest necessities in my small suitcase. I had arranged for my diary, letters and photographs to be sent home; and I left instructions that when my trunk from Tahiti arrived, it was to be sent home, too. I had with me my camera, though I was fully prepared that at some time or other it would be confiscated. This was because I had no liking for the Japanese and viewed them with considerable suspicion.

In the second class I was the only passenger. I had to myself a double-deck cabin in the stern, all the second-class deck space, the dining-room, and the lounge; and there were four Japanese stewards who had nothing else to do except to look after me. When I remarked upon this unaccustomed luxury to the tubby, round-faced purser, he laughed. 'Generally at this time of year we are full—but now no one likes us!' And he burst into laughter again as if the boycott was a huge joke.

We edged away from the wharf at noon, 2 April. Japanese music blared from the loud-speakers and passengers hurled coloured-paper streamers to their friends on the quay. In a few minutes we were out in the middle of the harbour of bays and passing slowly under the Bridge which all Sydney people refer to as 'our bridge'; and which every visitor gets bored to tears with because of the scores of times he's asked his opinion of it. My answer was always perfectly frank. I neither thought the harbour as beautiful as that of San Francisco nor the Bridge as fine as the Golden Gate.

I had my lunch alone. It was excellent, consisting of grilled thrush and Spanish chestnut pudding; and the first meal of some forty I had on the voyage at which no dish was ever repeated and which provided a standard of food unequalled by any British line. Always there was a menu in a cover of lovely Japanese coloured designs (different for each meal), and at this first lunch there was also a booklet, a guide to the Japanese language presented to me with the compliments of the NYK. I got busy with it in an effort to talk to the stewards. I was greeted with shrieks of merriment. My pronunciation was quite astray and they tried hard to improve it. So the game went on, until in a pause one of them, quite out of the blue (we hadn't mentioned politics), said in his best English: 'Japan so small and so full. Australia so big and so empty!' And then laughed in a merry way as if he'd said something very funny.

2

For ten days we hugged the Barrier Reef, never

out of sight of the Queensland coast, and passing islands so close that we could see the colour of the sea-birds perching on the rocks. A canvas bathing pool had been rigged up on the fore-deck, and in the blaze of the day I would cool myself in the water; when I got out it was so hot that I was dry in five minutes without touching a towel, and as I walked the deck it seemed that my feet were on hot coals. I would hang over the side and watch the porpoises, their brown bodies glistening in the sunlight, leaping and plunging in a hectic race to keep up with us; or I'd join the squat sailors in the stern who were throwing their fishing-lines in the churn of our wake.

I was allowed to wander pretty freely in the first class, making a friend there of an Australian marine engineer named Jefferies who was on his way to Hong Kong to take up an appointment as chief engineer of a newly-built coastal steamer. He was a huge fellow with a mouth like Joe E. Brown; and he had tales to tell of the Southern Seas that were not half exhausted after twenty days of his companionship.

One or two were about Errol Flynn. Flynn was adventuring around New Guinea when Jefferies first met him. Flynn was at the time recruiting natives for the New Guinea Gold Fields. Black-birding, it's called, and the price is £20 for every native who will accept a two-years' agreement to work in the mines. Flynn wasn't having much success until one day, in front of a Chief, he played the disappearing and reappearing coin trick—producing coins from behind his ears and out of his mouth, from the tummy of the Chief and the seat of his trousers. The Chief was amazed, quite certain it was a miracle. And so Flynn, taking advantage of the situation, held up the bamboo stick he had in his hand and explained that if the Chief had the stick, each time the moon was full he could do the same. The Chief forthwith took Flynn at his word and in exchange for the stick gave him fifty boys. Which meant a £1000 into the pocket of Errol Flynn.

At another time he wanted to make a film of the South Seas with Jefferies, but changed his mind when he bought a half-share in a Salamara hotel. Once he bathed naked for a bet on a Sydney beach and when a policeman arrived to arrest him for indecency he explained that a shark had bitten off his trunks; and so convincing was he that the policeman let him off.

There was a German aboard who, though an Aryan, was a refugee from the Nazis. In the sobriety of the day he would talk of his hate of Hitler. 'Only the youths are with him,' he said, 'we older people hate him. We felt last September that you should have called his bluff. We used to say: "If only Eden was Premier and not Chamberlain."'

But in the evening as he sat drinking beer

with Jefferies and me his Teutonic upbringing was too strong for him. 'England,' he would say, 'will be beaten in a few months if a war takes place with Germany within two years. She will be committing suicide. She is a dwarf compared with Germany's strength. Even her navy is not as powerful ... for Germany has secretly armed all her merchant ships so that her fleet is both more modern and larger than yours.' He was on his way to Manila, he told us, having left his wife and small daughter in Sydney. He had invested a large amount of his savings in an NYK ticket which he had paid for in Germany with the marks he couldn't take out of the country; and so he was using up the ticket by wandering around in NYK boats. He had already been to Japan and, *à propos* of this visit, he said to me one day: 'What a pity your people and mine can't get together—because it is in the East that the danger lies. The West will need all its strength to defend its existence.'

It was difficult to believe this when talking to the Japanese on board. They were gay and amusing companions and showed an astonishing naïvety in their efforts to be liked. Not having known any before, I was surprised to find that I felt as much at ease with them as with my own race. One among them was a young Consul official returning to the Foreign Office in Tokyo; he attempted to alter my anti-Japanese outlook.

'It is not easy for us in Japan to forget how

you took Hong Kong and established yourselves in other parts of China,' he said. 'Hong Kong became yours after a war caused by the refusal of the Chinese to allow you to import opium from Burma. You excuse yourselves by saying that that was long ago and two wrongs don't make a right; but you make no effort to make amends by returning the conquered territory to its owners. If you are like that, why shouldn't other nations expand as well?'

Such questions, if I want to be honest, I find difficult to answer. I can readily put myself in the place of a foreigner who boils with rage over our superior, sanctimonious attitude. And you'll find our behaviour in China, if you look into its history, quite shameless.

'You conveniently forget, now that you've condemned Japan as an aggressor nation,' he went on, 'that ever since the first Englishman landed in China, the Chinese have been trying to get you out. The memories of most of your people are so short that they do not remember that in 1927 five battalions of British troops had to be sent to Shanghai to restore order; and the Kuomintang published a declaration at the time to herald the "revolutionary struggle against British imperialism".'

I had to admit that my memory was very short, and that most of what he told me was new to me. In England we think of the Chinese as peaceful, easy-going people who love us as brothers; and as far as I was concerned I never even considered the possibility of the Japanese having a case for their actions. I was beginning to learn.

3

We spent a morning at Thursday Island, a weird shell of a place which once upon a time roared with the swash-buckling lives of pirates, pearl merchants, adventurers and gamblers. We'd left the ship in the outer bay and came to the wooden wharf by a launch manned by three coal-black aborigines. A half-dozen pearl luggers were anchored nearby, and we could see the little Japanese divers squatting on the decks; for the Japanese are easily the best pearl divers in these parts, a fact which is a never-ending source of chagrin to the Australians. But though pearl diving still goes on, there is none of the prosperity of the old days. The main street was like the deserted set of *Barbary Coast* I'd seen in Hollywood. The saloons that once were filled with noise and drinking, perhaps a score of them, were boarded up with faded signs of 'For Sale' nailed to the rotting wooden walls; and if you looked closely you could see dim posters proclaiming the date of the opening night of some Mae West of long ago. It was indeed a city of the dead.

As I was returning to the launch, I passed two men sitting on the kerb; I'd hardly noticed them until I heard them speaking the broadest

Scotch to each other. Their clothes were bedraggled to look at; and they wore caps which was strange for this part of the world. I stopped to have a word with them and they told me that they were brothers who, eleven years before, had left their native Highlands to seek their fortune in Australia. They'd done everything from gold-mining in Kalgoorlie to sheep farming in New South Wales, and they'd always remained together. Nor had either of them made a fortune. In fact, they just hoboed from Darwin, and for a month they'd been in TI without jobs. 'Only white trash can get jobs,' they explained. Now they had a plan to go to the Solomon Islands and they were hanging around for some boat which might be travelling that way. Maybe a month they'd have to wait, maybe six. They were a forlorn couple, and when I gave them five bob they were as grateful as starved dogs being given a bone.

For six days after leaving TI we touched no port, nor saw no passing ship. We were on a lonely track of the seas, sailing first through the Torres Strait, then the Arafura Sea south of Papua, and through the Banda Sea, dotted with islands of the eastern arm of the Netherland East Indies. No wind stirred the calm of the waters. Sometimes we'd see a giant shark leap at the sky from the depths and fall back with a splash that sounded like the crack of a whip. We'd twist and turn among the islands, so close to them that we would wave at the natives of the many that were inhabited. Often they'd sail out to meet us in their canoes with snow-white sails, and we'd throw at them anything that was handy; picture magazines, an old hat, or even cracked plates the dining-room steward found. Even more beautiful was it at night when the moon flooded the sea in silver and painted the islands in ghostliness. Jefferies said that he always considered this journey the loveliest sail in the world; and I would have agreed if I hadn't known Tahiti and Moorea and Bora Bora and Toopua.

At last we reached Davao, the hot and dirty port of Mindanao, the second largest island of the Philippines. It lies at the foot of a range of high hills and at the far corner of a deep bay that cuts into the island. Its streets are long and dusty, and its shops and bars are windowless like those of Panama. It is no advertisement for American colonization. There are only twenty Americans living there. They have apparently surrendered this rich and fertile island to the Japanese, of whom there are ten thousand in the district of Davao alone. This place is, in fact, a danger spot of the world. The Japanese, working much harder and more skilfully than the Filipinos, have collared the hemp and sugar plantations; and observers say that it is only a matter of time before they will be instructed from Tokyo to appeal to the Japanese armed forces 'to come to their help.'

This isn't likely to be before 1946, when the Philippines are promised complete independence by the United States. Then anything may happen, and now that the prospect of Japanese domination is facing them, the Filipinos are regretting like hell they've made such a fuss to become independent. It is difficult to see what they now can do about it. They aren't energetic enough to develop their country by themselves because, as a member of their Government put it: 'The Filipino does not work enough, he does not work continuously, he does not work scientifically ... and, what is worse, many Filipinos do not work at all.' Nor can they hope to defend it without the aid of America, and in the event of America not coming to their help the Japanese will not be able to resist the temptation of marching in with a 'New Order for the Philippines.'

We had a day and a night in Davao, loading hemp from lighters, and then we sailed up the coast to Manila. Japanese swarmed on the boat here, and we set off for Hong Kong with two hundred in the steerage and every cabin full both in the first and the second classes. My companion was a garrulous American of sixty years, with eyes that squinted at right angles to each other. In the three days and nights he told me of a score of shady incidents he'd been mixed up in, in Manchukuo and Japan; and he seemed to think that the Japanese wouldn't

228

want to see him any more. He'd been staying three months in Manila, and was on his way to Shanghai. A knapsack was his only luggage, and there were holes in his shirt, and a patch in the seat of his trousers. He earned a meagre living by teaching English. He gave me certain advice of the ways of the Orient. 'Chinks will nab anything they lay their damned hands on,' he said on the second morning, looking round to see no one was peeping through the porthole. 'See here, I keep my dough in this specially made strap ... on the groin.'

We crossed the China Sea uneventfully, arriving off Hong Kong in a dense fog. We hung around for a couple of hours, bleating like a lost sheep, until it lifted a little, and we could slowly nose our way through the mass of islands that guard the entrance of the harbour. We could see the gun emplacements and the barbed wire that zigzagged round the cliffs, and we were so close that we could see the Chinese written characters forbidding anyone to land. Outside the purser's office, and in other parts of the ship, there were notices forbidding anyone to take photographs. It was difficult to believe this was so. I counted thirty Japanese in the stern, all with their cameras, hurriedly snapping pictures of the fortress they would so like to possess. They showed a disregard to officialdom that, in Japan, would land a foreigner in gaol. When I was in Tokyo two American students were arrested for taking photographs of Yokohama from a Japanese liner. And the two contrasting incidents upheld my American companion's opinion of the nation: 'They grin like Cheshire cats in a foreign country and get away with murder. But in Japan they treat a foreigner as a criminal before he even thinks of a crime to commit.'

CHAPTER THIRTEEN

ORIENTAL KALEIDOSCOPE

To write of the Far East in a single chapter is as absurd as copying out the Bible on a penny stamp.

I found Hong Kong as complacent as Stratford-on-Avon; and this surprised me, as from a distance I'd come to the conclusion that at any moment the Japanese might attack it. There appeared to be no air-raid shelters, no plans to evacuate the population, and no talk that these precautions were necessary. When I asked what would happen if it was besieged, people shrugged their shoulders, saying: 'We'd last three months in any case.'

The fighting abilities of the Japanese were rated very low; and it was considered that the commanders, if faced by swiftly-changing tactics of British soldiers and sailors, would be as useless as aeroplanes without wings. So I asked Graham Barrow, Reuter's correspondent in Hong Kong, why, in that case, the Chinese were being beaten.

'The Chinese being beaten?' he replied. 'You won't find that idea among us who are covering the war.'

To a layman this was difficult to believe. All ports were in Japanese hands. Every big city had been surrendered—Peking, Shanghai, Nanking, Hankow, Canton. And the Government had taken refuge in Chungking, one thousand miles from Nanking, where they were when the war started. I would have thought that the Chinese were on the run; but what Graham Barrow had said I found to be the view of the greater proportion of European business men and newspaper correspondents I met.

Naturally, I tried to find out how it was, considering the circumstances, that China was going to win the war. But the answers were vague and conflicting. I would be told that the Chinese military leaders were soaked in graft, that they were incompetent, that they wouldn't co-ordinate with each other, and wouldn't take advice from any European adviser. At the same time, I would be told that the withdrawal was strategic, forcing the Japanese to lengthen their lines of communication, and enabling the Chinese to harass them day and night. I would be told that the Chinese were incapable of winning an offensive victory in the field, and yet the time would come when the Japanese would withdraw to the coast. To an outsider, who knew nothing of the Chinese character, it seemed that Graham Barrow and his friends were wishful thinkers. But when I was in Tokyo a Japanese diplomat put in a sentence what they were driving at. He said: 'When I was in Peking, last month, an old Chinaman whom I have long known came to me saying in all seriousness: "We Chinese know that your invasion of our country is only a passing phase of a century or so."' The remark cleared the fog in my mind. Even if in the next year or two there is a 'peace,' from the Chinese point of view it will only be a truce. It will not be the end of the war. They will reorganize their forces and strike again. They will give the Japanese no rest, no time to consolidate their gains. With the persistency of mosquitoes in a tropical swamp, they will bite and bite until in weary desperation the Japanese withdraw. Perhaps in ten years. Perhaps in a hundred. The time does not matter.

From the British outlook, if the army remains in power in Japan, it is best that the war should drag on and that stability does not come to China. Likewise from the French, or the American, or the Italian. An American merchant in Shanghai was one of several who explained to me why. 'Our trade,' he said, 'has of course suffered considerably, but we are at

232

least still keeping our heads above water. If the Japanese licked the Chinese, and if they were really able to organize the territory they occupy, it wouldn't be long before they turfed us out. After all, there is no military force to oppose them except a few hundred soldiers in Shanghai and a few score in Peking and Tientsin. Once they did, one couldn't expect America to send an expeditionary force to rescue us; and Britain obviously couldn't do much. Then, on the other hand, supposing the Chinese licked the Japanese, it would be silly to think they would be content with that. The Chinese are anti-foreigners, Japanese or Europeans, and they would soon swing round from their present policy of courting us to that of driving us away. We who have lived here for many years do not forget the Chinese boycotts and armed demonstrations against us. In 1937, during the Shanghai fighting, many were convinced, among them myself, that if Chiang Kai Shek's forces had succeeded in driving the Japanese into the Whangpoo, the Chinese would have swept through the International Settlement. Mind you, it was a very near thing. The Japs had only four thousand troops defending the Hongkew area against Kai Shek's army of fifty thousand. The Chinese even got through to the Bund, and it was only rank incompetence on their part that turned imminent victory into defeat. But it would be humbug not to admit we were thankful when

233

the Japs got the upper hand.'

2

My father came to my rescue in Hong Kong
with a cheque; and this considerably improved
my financial position, coupled with the
discovery that, before leaving for Japan,
through certain Chinese exchange dealers I
would be able to get 27 yen to the £1 instead of
the official 17. I stayed therefore a few days in
Hong Kong before taking an Italian liner up to
Shanghai. The liner was crammed with Jewish
refugees who were following the Russian influx
into Shanghai of twenty years before. They
were an ugly, pathetic sight. Their future was
as blank as a man who has been sentenced to
life imprisonment. Already ten thousand were
quartered in camps outside the International
Settlement in the Hongkew area, and prospects
of employment were practically nil. A
thousand of these, I was told, were
professional men but only two hundred had
found employment of any kind. The story of
how the Russians sank to accepting coolie
wages has often been told. Whether the Jews
will do the same remains to be seen. Their
trouble is made doubly worse by the already
large number of Chinese refugees in the
International Settlement. That they may
overcome their difficulties by cunning Jewish
methods is suggested by the story of a friend of
mine. He had a flat to let in the Avenue Haig,

and as flats are at a premium in Shanghai, he knew he could get a good price for it. When, however, a forlorn Jewish refugee, with his wife and four children, called on him and begged for a reduced rate, he was moved to pity and let them have it. A week later, having left behind a picture, he went back. Instead of the Jew in the flat, he found an American. And it transpired that the Jew, having got the reduced rate, went the same day to the American and rented the flat to him for a hundred dollars a month more.

Shanghai is a flat, dusty, smelly city, with a tense atmosphere; at any moment, as you walk along the street, you expect a hold-up and to hear the crack of shots. Danger, excitement and a certain romance is in the air. Ten minutes after the liner docked I was in a launch, talking to an American river police sergeant, on my way to the Customs. Suddenly he nudged me. 'See that guy with a coat over his arm?' His thumb pointed to a dark young Russian, as good-looking as a film star. 'I'll call him over. He's a pickpocket.' The young man answered the call. 'Had any luck today?' asked the sergeant. 'No,' answered the man, 'no luck at all. I have only just started.' He spoke good English and the sergeant let me talk to him. It seemed the most natural thing to talk of his exploits, despite the presence of the policeman. 'Sometimes,' he explained, 'I do quite well on this launch as the people go to the Customs. I

235

am one of a gang and we share what we collect.'
The sergeant laughed. 'Anyhow, come into the
lavatory. I'll have to search you. If, as you say,
you've had no luck, I'll let you go.'

Pickpockets, you see, are as insignificant
lawbreakers in Shanghai as cyclists without
rear lights are in England. The daily task of the
police is to deal with gunmen who operate on a
far bigger scale than ever was the case in the
wild days of Chicago. Several lose their lives
every year, and yet there is no national honour
attached to their bravery. They are serving an
International Settlement. They don't die for
their country.

Over four hundred Britishers are in the
Force. They're all sergeants, either detectives
or policemen, and they have about four
thousand Chinese under them. There are
White Russians and Sikhs as well. The Chief
Constable is Major Bourne, who won the M.C.
in the Great War. Two policemen patrol the
grounds of his home day and night; and his two
children can never go out without a guard for
fear of kidnappers. And yet, he and his wife
appear as indifferent to danger as if they were a
retired couple in Budleigh Salterton. I went
with them to the police sports. The stands were
crowded with Europeans and Chinese. Mrs
Bourne was to present the prizes, and just
before she mounted the dais to do so she said to
me: 'I often wonder what I would do if
someone on such an occasion as this tried to

shoot me.' The day before, the wife of a police sergeant was actually faced with this problem. She and her husband were in a tram in the Bubbling Well Road on their way to the cinema when a bullet smashed the window beside them. The sergeant was out of the tram in a second and was firing at a coolie that was running away. He missed, but after reporting the matter, the two of them went on to the pictures. The Chinese have a nasty habit of revenging themselves on the police for relatives that have been arrested (you can hire an assassin for a couple of pounds, it is said). Shortly before I arrived, the chief Chinese detective of the Force, a man named Lo, had been assassinated. He himself had been a bandit before he came over to the side of the law; and with him he had brought fifty thousand 'dudies' or followers, which is the other name for them. These 'dudies' looked upon him as their leader and acted as informers. For several years, since they were in every kind of Shanghai life, they were able to tip him off before any plan to kill him succeeded. He, however, had a girlfriend whom he liked to visit unaccompanied by his guards; and on one such visit his 'dudies' failed him. As he came away from her apartment he was greeted by a hail of bullets. A gang, whose leader he had arrested, had got their revenge.

The work of the police is made more difficult by the Japanese. A diplomat's patience has to be added to their qualifications. On the second day I was there a prominent British educationalist was killed, along with a Japanese sentry, as a result of a collision between his car and a Japanese-owned bus in the Japanese area of Hongkew. The man's wife and a British police sergeant were seriously injured and taken to hospital for treatment. They were at once put on the danger list, but this didn't stop a Japanese officer thrusting his way to where they were lying and interrogating them in an offensive manner. An assistant commissioner of the police tried to reason with him, whereupon the Japanese officer hit him in the face.

3

It is difficult to understand why the Japanese are so unpleasant in China. Vere Redman, who was *Daily Mail* correspondent in Tokyo and who has covered for his newspaper many phases of the war, says there are two Japanese nations; the one which is in China and the other which is in Japan. 'There must be something in the air of China that makes a Japanese into an unfeeling bully,' he told me, 'because there is no more courteous and friendly person than he when he is in his own country.' I discovered this for myself, and also that the great majority of the Japanese population are ignorant of the brutality and conceit of their army. And that the intelligent civilians who do know are ashamed. I had lunch in Tokyo one day with Yukichi Iwanaga who was head of Domei, the news agency, until he died a few weeks ago. He was responsible for the dissemination of Japanese news to the whole world, not only to Japan. He was on the same level as the Minister of Information. I was asking him why the Japanese people permitted their army to disgrace the nation, and he replied: 'They don't know of any of the beastly things that happen. It is my job to hide the truth, and I tell you, it disgusts me having to do it.' I remember he went on to talk about Hore-Belisha. 'I wish,' he said, 'we could get someone like that to turn out our generals.'

Look, for instance, at a little publicized example of their obnoxious activities in Shanghai. Stretching out of the International Settlement into the districts are roads which come under the jurisdiction of the Municipal Council; in other words it has extra-territorial rights over them. A hundred yards off the roads, the Japanese-sponsored Chinese puppets take over control. If, therefore, a crime is committed on one of these roads the criminal has only to run a hundred yards for him to be free from the pursuing Municipal Police; and it is very seldom that the puppet police ever catch him, let alone hand him back to the Municipal Police. Such lack of co-operation is alone enough to anger the Europeans; but it is made much worse by the practice of the Japanese to let opium dens flourish in these areas, while in the Settlement itself the Municipal Police naturally forbid them.

I was taken to one of these dens by Kenneth Selby-Walker, Reuter's Special Correspondent. Incidentally, never will I allow that my countrymen in far-off places are frigid and inhospitable. I didn't know Selby-Walker from Adam until I rang him up and introduced myself. He promptly came round to see me, and while I was in Shanghai he and his young wife continuously entertained me and went to endless trouble to assure that I saw all I wanted. Such friendliness I found whenever I met Englishmen during my journeys, and the coldness I had been led to expect to find in them I found only in Americans. But as I said, Selby-Walker took me to one of these dens.

It was not as sinister as I expected. The building was called 'The Hollywood,' off Jessfield Road. The chief amusement in it was bahjeu and roulette. The gambling was pretty high, and, to protect their customers against bandits, it had been necessary for the proprietors to have built two gun-turrets at either end of the outside of the building. One of the guards, we were told, had shot the other the night before by mistake. Inside, it was the size of a dance-hall, with paper partitions dividing one gambling room from another. At one end were the small rooms of the opium smokers, and the sickly, pungent smell of the opium pervaded the whole place. What I noticed most was the child labour. There were children of nine or so, hurrying to and fro like waitresses in a restaurant. Not only were they employed in the gambling rooms, but also in the job of preparing the pipes of the opium smokers. I looked in at one of these small rooms and saw a little boy, squatting beside an old Chinaman and stirring the sticky mess of opium in a bowl. It was an ugly sight. It didn't say much for 'The New Order in Asia' and yet, when I later told Japanese of what I'd seen they were frankly horrified. Sotomatsu Kato, for instance, who is now Ambassador at Large to China, and whom I met in Hsinking, said: 'I deplore such things as much as you do.' This was the diplomat's way of saying he blamed the army; but more of that later.

The notorious Shanghai night-life, after a quiet spell for the first year of the war, is now as wild as ever. Down in Blood Alley are the cheap, bawdy dance spots, where no evening passes without a fight. They are the Mecca of the American marines, the Italian, French, and British soldiers and sailors. I was down there one night, listening to a British Tommy. He had a hate against the Italians. 'Those bleeding Ities,' he said, 'their idea of an evening's sport is to go from bar to bar, 'alf-dozen together sort of thing, lookin' for one of us or a Froggie, and then tryin' to beat us up before our pals get wind of them.' Tourists are taken to the Alley so as to see a side of life that hasn't changed for thirty years. The Alley is where the word 'Shanghaied' was born. But there are dozens of other places to go to. Russian and Chinese dance restaurants with Filipino bands that have the rhythm and the music of first-class Western bands.

Or there are the small, soft-lighted clubs where only a piano plays, or a piano and a violin. Russian and Chinese dance hostesses sit side by side. The Russians are tall, and would be elegant if they were dressed in Parisian clothes; but as they are, they look drab, and tired of life. The Chinese, on the other hand, are small with exquisite figures, wearing the national dress in many coloured silks; close fitting, high collar, short sleeves, and a slit in the side of the skirt so, as they walk, you see a slim bare leg from the knee to the foot. At threepence a time you dance with them, the Russians gloomy and silent, the Chinese dumb and emotionless.

Brothels abound like public houses in Glasgow. The first evening in my hotel the house-boy asked: 'Want nicee Chinee ladee?' Out in the streets they were hanging about, always accompanied by an *amah*. This old lady might be the girl's real mother or she might have bought her as a child. At any rate, if you wanted the girl, you didn't discuss money matters with her; you argued with the *amah*.

The Russians were herded together in gloomy houses. The one I visited was kept by an elderly American woman, and the girls, over whom she presided like a nurse in a nursery school, were worn and fat and unappealing. She wasn't at all upset that I and my friend went away without being customers. 'You must come again,' she said cheerfully, 'all my girls are guaranteed clean. I haven't had a case of venereal disease for five years. On that occasion a policeman claimed he got ill from one of my girls. So I gave him £50 as compensation!' The brothels in Japan are licensed and supervised by the police. The Japanese have a realistic outlook towards sex. They do not pretend it does not exist, nor do they feel it should be indulged in furtively. The army in China, for instance, have girls following after them in groups as well organized as any military unit. It may seem funny to Western ideas, but it stops homosexuality and other vices which are inevitable when young men of any army are forced to live for a long time together.

4

The army, however, though it may be a platitude to say so, is the evil thing of Japan. Never having suffered defeat in war, it is puffed up with its own conceit, and is convinced that its duty is not only to fight for Japan but to rule it as well. It is responsible for assassination, insolence, bribery, and brutality; and whenever it is pricked by conscience it excuses itself by saying it represents the Emperor and he, being the Son of Heaven, can do no wrong. If the Emperor only knew what sins were committed in his name, he would probably abdicate. He is a fine man, who has already shown his dislike for the revolting methods of his soldiery, by standing out against the pact with Germany, whose soldiers have similar ways of behaving. It is said that he favours Japan coming to terms with the democracies; and there is no doubt of the presence of an influential group of statesmen who are in agreement with him. Such men, if they were in power, would be as honourable in their diplomacy as a British Government. They would respect our rights as conscientiously as we respected theirs. Honour, decency, and justice would be once again the policy of the Japanese people.

There are signs that this group of statesmen are increasing their power; the nation is growing tired of the vapid boasts of the army. A prominent Japanese diplomat talked to me of how Britain could strengthen their hand. 'Your country,' he said, 'have a knack of casting its friends into the arms of its enemies. Look at Italy. She has always been at heart a friend of yours, yet by tactless and useless acts, you drove her to the side of Germany. Same with Japan. Though you blame us for everything, I assure you the antagonism shown by our people towards you is a great deal owing to your clumsy diplomacy. For instance, since the war began you've lodged nearly a thousand complaints at our Foreign Office about damage done to your property in China. Every time, even if so much as a slate on a roof is damaged, your Ambassador calls with a note, stiffly worded with a hint of threats. Can you imagine how you would feel if America did this to you when you were engaged in a life and death struggle with Germany? You would boil with anger. And if America took no action to carry out her threats or see that her demands were settled what else would happen? You would lose respect for her word, just as we have lost respect for yours. For twenty years your country and mine were close friends and allies. The Japanese people are still at heart closer to Britain than to any other nation. If you would realize that, and would direct your policy towards strengthening the position of the moderates in Japan, rather than feeding the extremists, and by them I mean the army, with ammunition to use against you, your country and mine could become allies again, and our common interests established on a lasting basis.'

The mass of the Japanese people are obviously bitter towards us. Propaganda has made us the scapegoats for the army's failure to subjugate China. Even though the United

245

States, being in a stronger position than ourselves, has been able to be correspondingly firmer in her policy towards Japan, I didn't meet a single Japanese who was anti-American in the same way as he was anti-British. Rightly or wrongly, it was thought that Britain was to blame for America's firm attitude. And it was firmly believed that China would not be fighting if it were not for the support being given her by Britain. As Major Akiyama, the army spokesman, said to me in Tokyo: 'It is certainly true to say that at any rate the youth of Japan now feel their country is fighting Britain, not China.' That the Japanese feel so strongly about us, seems to suggest that perhaps we are a little to blame. Such a view was expressed to me by an Englishman who had lived a long time in Japan. 'It is a pity,' he said, 'that our Foreign Office hasn't been more realistic. They should have realized from the beginning that our position was extremely weak in the Far East. And instead of adopting a Palmerstonian attitude, they should have been clever enough to have kept on friendly terms with Japan while at the same time being friendly with China. After all, the Germans have done so; they have been supplying China with arms while coming to terms with Japan. Where they have succeeded, why couldn't we?'

5

I had hoped that my stay in Japan would be

made the more exciting by finding my movements were being shadowed. I went long walks down deserted streets and lonely parks, but never once caught sight of a suspicious-looking follower. Nor on my arrival at Kobe in the *Shanghai Maru*, a boat that was crowded with returning army officers and soldiers, was I even questioned at length; nor during my stay did I once discover that my baggage had been examined. The only time the police took any notice of me was after I'd been to the Soviet Embassy for my visa through Russia. As I came out through the gates, they took my name and address, and inquired my business. I was a little disappointed at this lack of attention.

For the most part, however, they're as suspicious of foreigners as mice of cats. You cannot, for instance, buy the Official Guide to Japan as produced up to 1933; the maps then printed might give secrets away. When, in a train, you're passing a port you might as well be in the Piccadilly Tube for all you can see; high boards beside the track hide the ships that might be there. A friend of mine bought picture postcards of Japanese aeroplanes in a stationer's shop; he was promptly taken to the police station as a potential spy. I wanted to have a look at one of the big cotton mills, but I was forbidden to do so because I might have discovered some secret process to take back to Lancashire. And then, of course, all foreign books and newspapers are strictly censored, so that on the bookstalls you can only buy the rosy Japanese point of view.

Thanks, however, to my friends in Domei, I was allowed to see a paper factory; and despite the fact that economic figures are forbidden to be disclosed by law, I learnt some wage figures that were interesting. For instance, in this factory which, like everything in Japan, was as clean as a dairy, the men worked eleven hours a day, seven days a week, for 1s. 6d. a day; and the girls, for the same length of time, at a 1s. a day. These figures in Western ideas are the next thing to slavery; and it seems impossible that anyone could work for such wages with a good heart. It is obvious, however, that under such conditions Japanese industry can turn out goods far cheaper than those of the Western world. It puts us in a hopelessly unequal position. We can and do, of course, impose high tariffs to bring them nearer the level of our goods, but that, after all, is only a synthetic trick of keeping our trade. Nor does it answer the question put to me by our Japanese industrialist: 'Isn't it wrong,' he asked, 'that you should deliberately keep away from your working people the kind of articles that at our prices are within their pockets, but at yours are beyond them?'

It puzzled me why the Japanese workers accept such working conditions. After all, they have scarcely any time for home life or recreation; and you would think they would get tired of their ceaseless labour. The answer lies in Shintoism. Shintoism is the worship for the Emperor, and it has the same meaning as the Nazis' worship for the State. It is a most convenient gag to suck the last drop of energy out of the population for the benefit of the Government. The factory girl at her 1s. a day is not working for herself; she is working for the Emperor. Every hour she is beside her machine she has spent to bring more glory to the Son of Heaven. Such a state of affairs is the answered prayer of industrialists the world over ... but how long is it going to last in Japan?

Education is the pride of the nation. It doesn't matter how poor a toddler may be, he goes to school; and, if he has brains, because of State-supported schools and universities he can go on learning till he is twenty-five and more. Not unnaturally this education is sowing the seeds of doubt in the minds of the young working class. Like in Britain in the middle of the nineteenth century, they are beginning to ask themselves why they should work so hard for so little profit. Mass action to improve conditions may be a long way off; but, with increasing regularity, news seeps through to the Europeans in the capital, of strikes that have to be quashed by the police; maybe these disturbances are straws in the wind of what is to come. While the war lasts and providing it doesn't last too long, Shintoism will maintain its power over the people, but afterwards who knows? Certainly in the minds of progressive Japanese a change in the way of things would not be unexpected. One of their best-known journalists said to me: 'The working class are being awakened. Not only by education, but by the cinema as well. They are at the same stage as yours were fifty years ago.' Then he added, with a disarming giggle, typically Japanese: 'Perhaps in ten years . . . we will be in the soup!'

6

Among the little things of Japan I'll remember, will be the pink, bare feet of the slum dwellers, as if they'd come straight from a hot bath; and the paradoxical sight in dustless, spotless Tokyo of men urinating in the gutters. There'll be the rowdy drunkenness in the streets off the Ginza at night. The feeling as you enter a shop, this being the exact opposite in China, that the salesman will not try to cheat you. The politeness of everyone. The European cooking which is as good as in Paris. How half the girls wear the national kimono and obi, and the other half Western clothes as chic as the girls in New York. The bells of the newspaper sellers. The enthusiastic audience at the embarrassingly bad 'leg show' at the Takarazuka Theatre.

I'll remember, too, the unshaven clerk at the Russian Consulate who kept me waiting a fortnight for my visa while he telegraphed to Moscow. The other Russian at the Intourist to whom I paid the £40 for my journey to Paris. The sleeping berths in the night train to Shimonoseki that were open without privacy on to the corridor. The *geisha* who had the one beneath mine, and the young officer who asked me to lend him my sponge. The clean grey kimono and slippers provided with each berth. The wash-place that had no door. The silent group in black, two old men and two old women, who the following day sat motionless at one end of the long carriage, each with a white square box on the knees—the ashes of their soldier sons killed in the war. The endless miles of plains and hills and valleys, no yard of which was uncultivated, resembling a vast kitchen garden. And then my last memory of Japan, the yells of: 'Banzai!' as loud as the yells of American college boys at a football match, that came from a troop train halted in the ill-lit station of Shimonoseki, as I hurried, a suitcase in either hand, with the bustling crowd towards the midnight boat for Korea.

CHAPTER FOURTEEN

THIS COUNTRY DOESN'T EXIST

Two beefy American marines scowled at me

when I reached my cabin. They were taking the diplomatic mail from Tokyo to the American Embassy in Peking. They had no wish to have a stranger in their company; and for some minutes they argued with the steward in an attempt to get me moved. They had no luck as the boat was full; so, taking no chances, one of them went to bed with the chain of the heavy-looking black bag locked round his wrist.

We parted at seven the next morning when we landed at Fusan. They took the train for Peking and I found myself the only European on the one for Mukden. My Trans-Siberian connection didn't leave for a week, and I'd planned to stop there a night or so and also at Hsinking, the Manchukuo capital, and at Harbin. The carriage was without compartments, like those of the London Underground. Each seat had been reserved and mine luckily was a corner one. It meant that for the following twenty-four hours I at least had the window to rest my head against. My legs, however, were painfully cramped as I had no more room than if I'd been sitting in a General omnibus, and if I stretched them even a little bit, they got entangled with those of the two passengers facing me. One was a quaint little Japanese who was off on a fishing holiday to some river near Mukden, and the other a fat, thick red-lipped Korean woman with rosy bare feet, a blue kimono and gold obi. Beside me, who, during the coming hours, persistently

252

overflowed into my own square foot of the seat, was the woman's husband. He looked like a bandit. Slits of eyes set in an oval, unshaven face; dirty yellow teeth, a smell like a latrine, and a black skull cap. He would snore loudly, and drop his stubbled face so that it rested on my shoulder. I had no alternative but to stick it out; and for the whole of that night I didn't get a wink of sleep.

The other passengers were mostly returning soldiers of the Kwangtung army, which is the watch-dog of Manchukuo. I had three of them sharing my table for dinner. They had only two bottles of Kirin beer between them, but it was enough to set them singing and to make them feel brotherly towards me. Arms were flopped round my shoulders, and the health of Britain was drunk, and by picking out isolated words from my Japanese dictionary I made a speech in praise of Nippon which resulted in prolonged cheers of 'Banzai!' Back in the carriage they shrieked songs which reminded one of the jungle, and which is the habit of Japanese when they're tight. Across the gangway in the four seats parallel to ours were three shy little *geishas* who giggled like schoolgirls whenever anyone spoke to them, and a Mongolian schoolboy who sucked oranges; and in other parts of the carriage were six Japanese of university age who would take it in turn to practise their English on me. It was exceedingly boring correcting their grammar, but I kept my patience. If you're in a foreign land you can do a lot of good for your country by being polite.

2

The railway wound in and out of the hills, past primitive villages with cottages round like big mushrooms and made of mud and straw; and men working in the rice fields dressed in long white coats like Finnish ski troops, and wearing tall hats like those of the witches in *Macbeth*. We passed Taikyu, and Keijo which is the centre of the Japanese administration of Korea; then through monotonous hilly country to Heijo that has a history dating back to 1122 BC. Darkness fell and I grew tired and bad-tempered. The carriage was smoky and stuffy. The bandit sagged against me, using me as a pillow, his skull cap falling off his head into my lap. The soldiers still made their noises. My legs ached. The bandit's wife snored. And the moment that I fell into a doze the train reached the Yalu river which divides Korea from Manchukuo, and we were at the frontier town of Antung.

Squat Manchu officials entered the carriage. They began their search of baggage and scrutiny of passports at the other end to where I was. They seemed to be casual, as if they wanted to complete their tiresome duties as quickly as possible. In ten minutes they'd looked at the baggage and passports of forty people without raising a query. And then they came to me. Four of them there were, oval yellow faces, black eyes blinking through inch-thick glasses, caps like Winston Churchill's yachting cap, and yattering together like monkeys in a zoo. I had already opened my suitcases and, as they foraged through my shirts and books and handkerchiefs, I pretended with my smiles that they were doing me the greatest favour by being so thorough. They scanned my books upside down and shook out my vests and pants for all to see. They took my camera to pieces and told me to empty my pockets. And having spent a quarter of an hour in doing this one of them began, in English, to ask me questions, but in such a parrot fashion that I was sure that he neither understood the questions he asked nor the answers I made. 'Where are you going?' 'What have you written for your paper?' 'Where were you educated?' 'What is your father's profession?' 'Why are you going to Russia?' and a whole lot of others. When they seemed to have finished I went out on to the platform to walk up and down in the darkness. The cross-examination had been easier than I'd expected. This was due, I thought, to my willingness to help and my care not to show impatience; after all, Custom Officials are only doing their job and the point of resenting their investigations, as many travellers do, seems to me pointless. And as I was thinking this, the English-

255

speaking little man stopped me, saying: 'Come back to the carriage, please.' He led me not to my seat, but to half-way down the carriage, so that when he stopped everyone had a chance to watch and be impressed by his mastery of English. He waited for the silence of his audience as a *prima donna* waits before beginning her song. The eyes of Mongols, Koreans, Japanese soldiers, and *geishas* were fixed on us. The sense of their expectancy that a European was going to be made a fool of filled the carriage with the same reality as the smoke and the stuffiness. He then began. 'Where are you going?' 'What have you written for your paper?' 'Where were you educated?' 'Why are you going to Russia?' 'What is your father's profession?' . . . All the questions he had asked before. I had no alternative but to answer them pleasantly. He was obviously anxious for me to lose my temper, and I refused to oblige him. And when he came to the question: 'What do you think of China?' I made an obscene snort which made our audience roar with laughter and so pleased the little man that he shot out his hand, saying: 'Goodbye and good luck!'

3

For seven more hours I sat cramped in my seat. I got no sleep, and when at last we arrived at Mukden, I felt that if I lay down on a bed I wouldn't get up for twenty-four hours. I bundled my suitcases in a droshky pulled by an

256

emaciated horse, and set off at one mile an hour for the Yamoto Hotel. I arrived there, only to find it full. Not a room to be had. I went to another hotel. The same result. I was told that they weren't Japanese that filled the rooms, but Germans. They swarmed everywhere. Engineers, insurance agents, journalists, motor-car salesmen. And after the second hotel had turned me down I was advised to go to a third hotel called the 'Kleining' that was run by a German. There I was shown a room, but I hadn't been in it five minutes before the Chinese boy knocked at the door and said he'd made a mistake. 'You're English,' he said, 'not allowed here.' I refused to go before I had a bath and a shave, and having made myself look a little more presentable, I set off to see the British Consul.

Perhaps I should remind you that Britain doesn't recognize Manchukuo, and that, therefore, our Consuls at Mukden and Harbin are not officially there; nor is the country itself, which the Japanese, in nine years, have transformed from being corrupt and bandit-ridden into being safe and civilized. Thus, thanks to this ostrich-like policy of ours, Britain has few interests, which results in the Consuls having correspondingly little to do compared with Consuls elsewhere. It couldn't, therefore, be on the plea of overwork that the Consul at Mukden was unable to offer me a cup of tea or a cigarette; or, since it was lunchtime, invite me to his table. After talking to me for a few minutes he made no secret of the fact that I had interrupted the peaceful routine of his day, and taking the hint I went away. It was the first time in my travels I'd come across the music-hall example of an Englishman's manners in a far-away country.

Since there was no room for me in Mukden, the only thing to do was to take the train to Hsinking. Here again I had difficulties. You have to reserve your seat on the crack 'Asia' express, and I found that every seat had been reserved. Luckily a young German overheard me at the booking office and he explained that if I bought a platform ticket no one would stop me going on the 'Asia' platform; and, once there, I could get on the train and pay my fare when the ticket collector came round. He said that the collector might be angry, but if he was I had no need to worry; the 'Asia' went non-stop to Hsinking, so he couldn't turn me off. I took the German's advice and, beyond a few cross words from the Manchu collector, the journey passed off without incident. It was a strange train to find oneself travelling in; streamlined and air-conditioned, with a lookout car for the first class like those of the crack American trains. There was a fair sprinkling of Europeans, but the majority were Japanese business men and soldiers; and it was odd to find in the dining-car, amongst all this yellow, two exceedingly pretty White Russian girls as waitresses. Still odder was the patrol of six Japanese soldiers, who, with fixed bayonets, continuously walked up and down the train. Such patrols are on every train in Manchukuo, not because there are frequent attacks, but because the Japanese believe that it is best to take no risks. We got into Hsinking after dark, where once again I was to find the only hotel full. I was tired beyond belief and had no care where I went; and finally I came to rest in a Japanese *ryokhan* on the top floor of a house that had a dirty staircase leading up to it like that of a Whitechapel office building. Before entering I had to take off my shoes and put on slippers, and then I discovered my bed was a mattress on the floor with crumpled, used sheets; and the room itself was an inside one with no windows. Even so I slept for twelve hours.

4

Japanese like to say that Manchukuo is to Japan as Egypt is to Britain. Both the smaller countries, they say, are independent, both have their own Royal house, and both are dependent on the bigger countries for protection. This, however, is wishful thinking on their part, for to say that Manchukuo is any degree independent is a pure myth. True they have a Manchu Emperor and the titular heads of Government departments are Manchus, but to think these gentlemen have any power is sheer nonsense. Each department has an Under-Secretary of State who is a Japanese and who makes the decisions; and the Manchu Prime Minister is himself subject to the control of the Director of the General Affairs Board, a Japanese called Naoki Hoshino, who tells him what to do. Then in the departments themselves all the best jobs go to Japanese. According to John Gunther, in the Department of Public Peace 82 per cent of the personnel is Japanese; in the General Affairs Board 72 per cent; in the Foreign and Home Office 63 per cent; in the Courts 87 per cent; in the Bureau of Capital Construction 88 per cent; in the Metropolitan Police Board 65 per cent; in the Department of Public Welfare 61 per cent; and in the provincial governments at least 60 per cent. It can hardly be said, therefore, that Manchukuo to Japan is like Egypt to Britain.

Why the Japanese should maintain this pretence of being innocent 'lookers-on' is difficult to understand. It is, however, an incredibly naive attempt to curry favour in foreign countries, an attempt they are repeating in China with no better success. With the passionate sincerity of crusaders, they believe their method absolves them from being branded as aggressors and conquerors; and they are at a loss to understand why countries other than Germany and Italy do not agree with them. It is not as if in Manchukuo they have something to be ashamed about, as if they were bad conquerors who wreak vengeance on the conquered like the Germans in Poland; Britons and Americans who, conveniently forgetting the history of their own countries, cry out from afar that Manchukuo should be given back to the Chinese, might alter their opinions if they took the trouble to discover for themselves what the Japanese have achieved in nine years.

Sitting in a corner of his long room which overlooks the grounds of the Emperor's Hsinking palace that is taking five years to build, Naoki Hoshino talked to me in broken English about their achievements. 'First,' he said, 'we had to bring law and order to the country. We found the only way to do this was to make every village a walled fortress. The inhabitants work in the fields by day and return to safety at night. And thus the bandits, unable to get food or ammunition, either give up being bandits or retire to the mountains. By this method we have practically wiped out banditry. And another thing that has helped us is the development of roads and railways. In 1932 there was a thousand kilometres of railways; in 1938 there was ten thousand. In 1932 there was three thousand kilometres of roads; in 1938, fifty-one thousand. At the same time we have set about to educate the masses. We are opening schools everywhere. In 1932 six hundred and sixty thousand attended primary schools; in 1938, one million five hundred thousand. In another five years all these figures will be doubled.'

The figures are certainly impressive. The production of them also cost a mint of money. It is estimated that £140,000,000 will have been invested in the country by 1942, and a cash return on the money is still a long way off. As Hoshino frankly said to me: 'We have no money to pay for goods we buy from foreign countries. We can only barter.' This suits Germany, who is providing the machinery to develop the resources; resources that are so extensive that no one, not even the Japanese, knows the sum total. It certainly contains large deposits of coal and iron, tremendous timber regions, a considerable amount of gold, excellent agricultural land, and soya beans that vary in their utility from being food to the Chinese and Japanese to being fuel, fertilizer, soap, and a hundred other things to industrialists. One important product the country lacks is oil. Japanese prospectors are exhaustively searching for it, and although a field has been discovered, it is only a very small one. Western powers should certainly pray that the prospectors meet with success, because if oil is found in Manchukuo, Japan will no longer look hungrily at Borneo and the Netherlands East Indies.

5

The problem that hangs over Manchukuo like the sword of Damocles is Russia. Japanese make no secret that they're terrified that Russia may attack; just as they make no secret that when they have firmly entrenched themselves in Manchukuo they intend to attack themselves. Sotomatsu Kato, who, as I've already said, is now Ambassador to China, and who, when I was in Hsinking, was Counsellor of the Japanese Embassy, said to me: 'The Russians have a magnificently equipped army which at the moment we have no wish to fight; though we have learnt from Russian soldiers who have deserted to us that the morale among the troops is not high.' The truth is that the Russian army is highly mechanized and the terrain of Manchukuo is favourable to such warfare; but the Kwangtung army, though it is supposed to be superior to the Japanese army in China, is hardly mechanized at all.

I got a taste of the nerviness of the Japanese when I arrived in Harbin. My arrival coincided with the first of three nights of black-out and ARP exercises. I hadn't been in my hotel half an hour when a Japanese sergeant and a White Russian acting as an interpreter called on me. They asked the same silly questions as the Manchu on the train, but in addition they tried to discover the hidden reason why I had landed in Harbin the very evening when these ARP exercises were taking place. Apparently, they thought I had come all the way from London to learn what Harbin looked like without lights. And during the following three days I had a suspicion, for the first time since I'd set foot on Japanese territory, that I was being followed.

When the old Chinese Eastern railway was still in Russian hands (the Russians sold it to the Japanese in 1934, after having given it partially back to the Chinese ten years before that), Harbin had the reputation of being the richest and gayest city of the Orient. Today it is a dead end of poverty. You still can see the large mansions and the impressive bars and hotels; but their walls are cracked and unpainted, and window-panes are broken. It has an air of faded, battered prosperity; like a man who was once rich but who now, though still wearing his fine clothes, stands begging, beaten by the wind and the rain, in the gutter. There is no hope in the hearts of the White Russians who live there. Even if they had money, they could not take it out of Manchukuo; for the Japanese forbid them doing so. They cannot therefore even make the journey to Shanghai or Tientsin, which towns, strangely enough, are the Mecca of most. One feels sorry for the drawn-faced and haggard elderly men and women, but it is the girls one really pities. There are many of them in the shops and the cafés working at coolie wages;

and they are pretty and astonishingly cultured, speaking perhaps French, English, and Japanese besides their native language. They have no future, and not much of a present. They're lined and old before they're thirty. And they don't even have the advantage of their sisters in Shanghai of becoming prostitutes; for in Harbin there is no one to pay them.

CHAPTER FIFTEEN

PRELUDE TO HELL

I left the sad, gloomy town on the first day of June. The train rattled for eight hours across the monotonous plains to Manchouli. We passed one after another of walled villages, and concrete pill-boxes guarding the ends of bridges. At each station, as we arrived and as we departed, the stationmaster and the soldiers on the platform stood at the salute, as if the Emperor himself was among the passengers. At Hailar, soldiers came into the compartments and drew the blinds, then stood in the corridor with fixed bayonets and the door open, so that we should not spy on the Japanese secret fortifications that border Siberia. They had forgotten the lavatory, however; and I went along there. As a result I

265

couldn't understand why they were making such a fuss. All I could see were endless miles of undulating plain, and, once or twice close to the railway, I saw several Mongol nomads on tough long-haired ponies and wearing their orange cloaks and sheep fur caps.

Across the frontier it was different. I could have understood the Russians wishing to hide from the gaze of foreigners the gun emplacements, the aerodromes, the trenches, the fields of barbed wire, that stretched all the way inland to Lake Baikal. Yet, they neither made us pull down the blinds nor did they patrol the corridor. We might have been in a train in England, so free were we. Though before we got into it we had trouble. At Manchouli the Japanese put us through the usual questions, adding one particularly naive one: 'Are you going to speak favourably of Japan when you're in Europe?' I answered I'd do my best, but I added that I'd take away a better impression of Japanese rule if they forbade the sale of forged bottles of Johnnie Walker whisky at the station bar; for, just previously, I'd been offered a bottle of the said brand, same size, same coloured labels, but with the name spelt 'Johnnie Wacker'. Having been dealt with by the Japanese, we now had to face the Russians. We got with our luggage into the Trans-Siberian train which took us in ten minutes to Otpor, the Russian frontier town. Out we had to get and once again go

266

through the performance of having our luggage searched and of being asked silly questions. My camera was sealed, together with the suitcase I wasn't going to need during the seven-day journey to Poland; and my money counted so that I couldn't indulge in any currency tricks. And when they had finished with me, and finished too with the score of other Europeans, men and women, who were my travelling companions, I got back into the train and waited for two hours after the appointed time of departure before the train started.

2

I was travelling 'soft' class, which is the Russian equivalent of our second; and at first sight it looked as if I was going to be very comfortable. Admittedly the carriage was so old that one of my companions had travelled in a similar one in 1911, but the compartment was the size of an English first-class one; and if, as I imagined, only one person was going to share it with me I had no reason to grumble. Most of my companions—they were Shanghai business men and their wives, British, Swedish, French, and German—were travelling first class; two or three 'hard' (the bunks are of wood) including an Irish woman missionary who had taught for twelve years in a school near Mukden; and four others like myself who were 'soft'. When the train steamed out of Otpor, no

267

one had appeared to share my compartment, and since my fellow Europeans were all fixed up, it meant that at some future station I would be joined by a Russian. With a certain misgiving I wondered what sort of a Bolshevik he would turn out to be.

I was unduly optimistic to expect only one. In the early hours of the following morning the train pulled into Chita, the town where one section of the Trans-Siberian railway branches to Vladivostok; and I awoke to find the dirty, sullen car-attendant shaking my shoulder and telling me by signs that he was going to make four berths in my compartment by pulling out the backs of the two lower ones. Without much pleasure I watched him fixing them, and then with still less (the space between the two pairs of berths was no bigger than that of an English third-class sleeper), I made room for two uniformed soldiers, an old woman of seventy with a shawl round her head, and a pretty little girl of four. They gave me no greeting and in fact, except for the little girl who stared, they took no notice of me. As they brought in their luggage, I clambered to one of the top bunks, deciding that I would be more independent there than in a lower one. For a long time I tried to go to sleep, but when finally I succeeded, I was soon awake again; for the little girl lying with her grandmother in the berth beneath mine was crying out in a small agonized voice: 'Mamma! Mamma!' She was going to do this regularly every night all the way to Moscow.

I paid for my meals by coupons which I had bought with my ticket; I got what they called first-class coupons as opposed to second class, since I was told that with them I could indulge in an endless supply of caviare besides having a bottle of mineral water a day. As it happened the caviare ran out on the third day, and as far as mineral water was concerned I never even saw a bottle. The meals were invariably late, sometimes as much as two hours, and when they arrived they never varied from either leatherlike steaks or tough, stringy chicken. Black bread with two pats of butter accompanied them, and at dinner there was cheese; though you were warned that if you took it, you wouldn't be allowed to have eggs for breakfast next day! My comrades in the compartment never went to the restaurant car, buying their food instead at the stations we stopped at. And I would lie in my bunk, my nostrils filled with the smell of garlic and fish, that seemed to be their favourite dish.

Most of my time I spent in my bunk. There was little else one could do. I would lie there in a doze, with the train jerking and rattling like a motor-car that has no tyres. I couldn't speak to my comrades as there was no language to speak to them in. But we used to smile politely at each other, and one of the soldiers used to loan me his newspapers, so that I could look at

269

the pictures. They were ruddy, fresh-faced, decent-looking young men with curly, dry, brown hair which they had an almost feminine interest in combing; one of them used to join me and the little girl, who was called Alla, in a game of hide-and-seek up and down the corridor. There were many children on the train. They were extraordinarily attractive and healthy-looking, and they had no fear of strangers; and the hours would pass in hectic games with them. It didn't seem possible that they would grow up like their sullen, pinch-faced mothers and fathers who looked as if they were fifty when they were thirty.

Every station we arrived at was crowded. We would look at the people as one does animals at a zoo. 'They seem to be in a better state than five years ago,' said an Englishman who had done the journey before. But that was scarcely a compliment. Their clothes were like the rags that film producers dress the crowds in in films of the French Revolution, and their faces had the same grim, smouldering hardness. Look as carefully as we could, we never saw a smile nor heard a laugh. Outside each stationmaster's office there was a large glass picture-case containing photographs of both men and women of fierce, criminal types; or what we thought were criminal types. But when we asked a Russian on the train who could speak English whether he could discover what crimes they had committed, he looked sternly at us.

'The photographs,' he said, 'are of those who have earned honour in their town by working harder than their comrades.' The stations were dirty and battered-looking, as if they'd been waiting ten years for a new coat of paint. And they were surprisingly small. Omsk, for instance, had but three platforms, smaller, therefore, than Wimbledon Underground station. Irkutsk had four. And yet these are two of the chief towns in the Soviet. Still stranger was the sight of Sverdlovsk, which was the scene of the murder of the Tsar, though in those days it was called Ekaterinburg. We reached it as dawn was breaking. I was woken up by a large woman who was taking the bunk vacated by one of the soldiers who had got out. She was standing by the window, hissing sobs, and in the half-light I could see her shoulders heaving up and down. And then through the window I saw her lover, a huge man in a heavy coat with fur collar and cap, standing looking at her, grimly silent. The pair of them stood like that for the half-hour we were in the station; and for the life of me I couldn't understand why they didn't prefer to stand by the carriage and talk.

As for myself, I pulled on my shoes and went out into the cold early morning for a stroll. There was a pale light behind the black of the Ural Mountains that surround the town, and a pall of smoke lay over the roofs and about the tall chimneys of the factories. Here was the centre point of the wealth of Russia, and from this junction was despatched to the four corners of the country thousands upon thousands of tons of coal and minerals. One would have thought, therefore, to see a station and rolling stock worthy of their importance. Yet the station, like Omsk and Irkutsk, was no bigger than that of an English small town; and the wagons, passenger carriages, and engines that were halted in the sidings were the kind that disappeared from the Great Western before the Great War. I do not see how Germany can make use of them. They are like ancient Parisian *fiacres* which, if they were loaded too heavily, would collapse. Even their Russian masters have found their age a hopeless drawback in their attempts to put the Russian railways on an organized basis; so one can hardly expect the Germans to fare any better. True, the Germans are fine organizers, but no amount of organizing can bring modernity to ancient trucks; and it's the rolling stock that is the root of the Russian transport problem. And then, of course, even if the Germans had them to spare, they cannot bring their trucks to Russia because of the difference in the gauge. Whatever the German propaganda machine would like the world to think, it will take years, besides costing millions of pounds, before materials to Germany can be transported in an amount commensurate to the need.

3

And then Moscow. We arrived at ten on a Sunday morning; but I was awake at daybreak, and got up to stand in the corridor to watch the flat, outlying country, and to notice with surprise that soldiers stood with fixed bayonets on every bridge the train passed. I had my last shave in the dirty lavatory at the end of the corridor; and listened for the last time to the raucous sound of music and propaganda that screeched from the loudspeakers which were fixed at intervals along the carriage. The Russian Intourist representative had warned us that the waitresses and car-attendants would not accept tips; and this was true if you offered them anything when one of their comrades was present. It wasn't true however when they were alone. They took what they could get.

We had fourteen hours before the train left for Warsaw and we were all taken, shepherded by Intourist officials, to the Hotel Metropole by Underground. The Moscow Underground is the pride of the Soviet; and admittedly if one stayed in it and didn't go above ground one would be impressed by the achievements of Communism. The trains are as good as the Piccadilly Tube, and the stations miniature marble palaces. But they only make the cobbled streets and the ugly buildings the more dreary and drab by contrast; and then, of course, they make the Hotel Metropole (the

Ritz of Moscow) look as dilapidated as a disused cotton mill. My first meal there was interrupted by the rain that dripped from the glass dome of the huge dining-hall on to my table. One naturally had to wait for an hour between each course; but the time passed quickly enough because of the amusement one had in watching at the other tables what in fact was a cartoonist's conception of Bolsheviks come to life. Moustaches, those peculiar shirts, coupons, and all.

As soon as I reached the hotel, I rang up Denny, who's been Moscow correspondent for the *New York Times* for five years. And while I was waiting for him to come round, I went out for a walk; though with dramatic seriousness the Intourist official warned me I should not go without a guide for fear of the Ogpu asking for my passport. I saw the great walls of the Kremlin, and the Red Square seemed a quarter of the size I expected it to be; and many shops whose windows were bare of goods. When I got back, Denny was waiting for me. We sat down in the lounge, and had been there but three minutes when he leant across to me, whispering: 'Say, one of the boys has just sat down beside you. We'd better go out into the car.' It was very film-like, very exciting, and very absurd. I laughed as I sat in the car beside him. 'When you've been here as long as I have,' he said, 'you can smell an Ogpu boy a mile off. Do you know all the contacts and friends in official circles I knew five years ago are now dead or missing? Do you blame me for feeling nervy?' He took me a sight-seeing drive round the city, and talked meanwhile about the Soviet. 'Heaven knows why you Britishers are trying to get a pact with them,' he said, 'your Foreign Office must be damned badly informed or else they'd know the country is dead rotten. Wages are going down and cost of living going up. Do you know the average wage is now lower than it was in Tsarist times? And production and transport is so bad that the people don't know from one winter to the next whether they're going to have enough food to fill their bellies. Stalin, I can assure you, is not playing your game. Supposing you find yourselves fighting the Nazis, he certainly won't come to your help whatever pact he's signed, unless Russia is attacked. It's absolutely impossible for Russia to wage war ... such a thing would irreparably dislocate production throughout the country, and then it would be only a question of time before there was revolution. Who the leader of it would be, I can't say. Stalin has been very thorough in his purges.'

What has happened since has proved how phoney were the negotiations between us and Stalin. And now, thank heavens, it is Hitler who has to deal with his trickery.

I, in my turn, had to deal with the trickery of one of his subjects on my return to the hotel.

The Ballet was performing at the Opera House, and though all tickets at the box office had been sold, I was informed that if I went along to the entrance I would find people auctioning them, in the manner of Covent Garden touts. I went to the exchange clerk and asked if he could change £2 into roubles. I explained what I was going to do, and asked him whether, if after all I couldn't get a ticket from a tout, he would give me back my £2. He said he would.

I ran across the square to the Opera House, but finding the touts were asking too much money, I hurried back again. I wasn't away more than ten minutes; but when I asked the exchange clerk for my £2, he looked blandly at me. 'It is against the law. I cannot do it,' he said in English. It was useless reminding him of his promise, or calling the manager of the hotel, or demanding the head of the Intourist Bureau to do something for me. They all looked woodenly at me, obstinately repeating it was against the law to hand the money back to me. At length, I became so angry that I cared neither that I was in the land of the Ogpu, nor that I was in the public lounge of the Metropole. I told them exactly what I thought of them, their damned Trans-Siberian railway, and the wretched mess they'd made of their country. And as the people in the lounge began to stop their chatter and watch, I finished off with the sentence: 'You live in the most uncivilized, uncouth country in the world.'

276

Not a very gentlemanly scene; yet I'm glad I
made it.

4

The loss of the £2 was a bad blow to my
finances. I now had only £7 to last me to
London, and I wanted to stay both in Warsaw
and Berlin. I reckoned that since that day long
ago when I'd set out for Southampton and
New York I'd spent £502; so that I'd collected
£59 from gifts and earnings during the course
of the journey. I'd had good value for my
money, but the lack of a little more had many
times been irksome. Perhaps I should have
earned more and that I was lazy not to have
done so; yet gathering stories entails capital
expenditure and this I couldn't afford to risk
unless I was certain the article would be sold. It
is very difficult to arrive in a strange town and
begin immediately to earn a living. If you're
ready to stay a long time, you may pick up a
routine job; but if you're only passing through,
it is next to the impossible to find a temporary
one. The days of the wandering adventurers
are gone for ever. The world is too cluttered up
with labour regulations and laws forbidding
travellers to land in countries without first
proving to the authorities they have enough
money to support themselves.

Entering Poland was like entering a farmer's
house after a visit to the pigsty. The moment
we crossed the frontier at Stolpce we found a

station that was painted snow white, well-fed looking peasants, and railway officials who were smartly dressed and obliging. The train, too, was as fine as the Royal Scot. And when a splendid-looking young officer in a flowing cloak and three-cornered cap gave me an example of Polish politeness by saluting me and asking if he could share my compartment (it was empty but for me) I felt delight that Poland was our ally; the pride of the Poles for their country seemed to me to be physically alive, and each individual wanted to show it off to a stranger. I remember a sentence of the young officer's as I said goodbye to him at Warsaw's station. 'When we fight,' he said, 'we will not be fighting for riches. We will be fighting for the lanes and fields of Poland.'

After I'd booked my room at the Europesci off the Pilsudski Square I looked for a journalist who would short cut my study of the political situation. And I was lucky to find Alex Small in the hotel, roving European correspondent of the *Chicago Tribune*. His views were brief and to the point: 'Hitler ought to have pulled the chain the day he marched into Prague,' he cracked, 'now whatever he does won't catch the Western Powers napping. He's sure to come into Poland, and there's nothing to stop him. The Polish staff are so damned slow-witted that they'll be running round in circles. Do you know they still think a cavalry division can beat a motorized division?

They've got no defences around Warsaw, no system of air raid precautions, and not even an air raid shelter. For the past week I've been pestering the authorities to tell me what they're going to do in the event of an attack on Warsaw, and all they do is to look wise and murmur: "Everything is prepared." Hell, when Germany starts, I give them five days before they've captured the city. France and Britain will turn the war into a long-drawn-out affair, and Germany won't be able to stand it. She won't get any support from Italy. I've just come from there, and the country is in a mess and will remain so for years. But mark my words, if you get tied up with Russia God help you. She'll double-cross you at the first opportunity. Your Government's crazy to be dickering with her.'

I had been for so long a far-off spectator of the European scene that I had grown accustomed to viewing it with the same dispassion as one does the pieces of a chess-board. The fear that chilled men had for me been dimmed by distance. War belonged to history, not to the present; not to me and my friends and the places I knew and loved. But, as Small talked, I felt myself slipping back into reality, as if I were forsaking the escape of a dream for the cold facts of the day; and as the winds of fear blew through my heart I remembered a scene that I'd been a part of, a long, long time ago.

I remembered the lagoon, cool and serene in the midday sun, dotted occasionally by the canoes of the fishermen, and stretching its turquoise calm towards the reef where the waves rolled in a thin white line; and then, in the distance, the misty outline of the Presqu'Ile of Tahiti. Old Gibbins, his moustache bristling white and furious with a curl like the Kaiser's, was beside me on the verandah, the two of us sipping the milk from coconut shells. A man of the world he once had been; he'd won honour in battle and served his country well. But I remembered the words he used, as he told me of his renunciation of the thing called civilization. 'There'll always be rivalry and bitterness and distrust between nations. They have the tortured minds of the inhabitants of Bedlam. There is no rest, no peace. I tell you, sir, when I was part of the world I was the same. My mind was like a bit of refuse on a rubbish heap. I saw no light and I myself was confusion. But here, from this spot, I see that world as if it were a glass bowl, and inside are the fishes swimming round and round, without end and without meaning.'

5

Warsaw had a happy, Ruritanian atmosphere in those days. Officers in splendid uniforms strode along the streets. Women were smartly dressed, and children looked clean and healthy. Food in plenty filled the shops, and the cabarets at night were packed. The antiquity of the buildings and the churches brooded a peace over the city; and the old bridges, across the Vistula, a quiet loveliness. I could not have believed that within two months they would be a shamble of ruins. Nor, when I left the city in the train for Berlin, could I believe that the rolling fields and snug farmhouses we passed could so soon have been turned into a battlefield. In all that I saw there was something permanent, something so good and solid that it didn't seem possible that the evil in man could touch it.

There were no complications facing me at the German frontier. I was neither questioned nor was my baggage searched. Someone, a few stations later, came in with a 'Heil Hitler' and sat down. I was taken so much by surprise that I said 'Heil Hitler' too. When I told the story to a friend in Berlin, he said: 'When they do that to me, I answer "God Save the King"!' I followed his example on the next occasion. Another passenger was a well-dressed middle-class woman who told me she had two sons in the army. But she added a sentence which was to be several times repeated to me while I was in Germany. 'None of us want war,' she said, 'we do not want our loved ones killed ... *und der Führer, er weiss das!*'

I didn't get the opinion that the Führer shared the same view when I saw the Unter den Linden and the Wilhelmstrasse next morning.

Paul of Yugoslavia was arriving on a ceremonial visit, and huge flags, alternately Nazi and Yugoslav, hung at twenty-yard intervals from every building. Aeroplanes roared over the roofs. Steel-helmeted troops rushed about in lorries, and high Nazi officials raced hither and thither in black open Mercédès cars. For five hours before the procession I wandered among the crowds watching the legions of marching girls and boys who had been called from the schools to swell the chorus of cheers with their unbroken voices. Bands were spaced at hundred-yard intervals, fat-bellied, big-mustachioed trumpet players, and a huge fellow to beat the big drum. Little flags were handed out to all and sundry by smooth young party men. Black-shirted storm troopers with magnificent physique lined the streets, each alternate one facing the crowd. And yet despite this pomp and circumstance, all of which I had read so often about before, there was an atmosphere of goodwill that was unexpected. Jokes among the storm troopers, bursts of laughter from the crowd when a civilian lost his way and was escorted across the cleared street by a policeman, and remarks such as: 'Oh, dear, how much longer have we to wait?' When at last the great moment arrived it was over in exactly thirty seconds. First Hitler and Paul flashed by, after the manner of: 'That's Shell ... that was!' and then followed, in speedy succession, Ribbentrop with a nasty, self-satisfied grin on his face; Goering, red and bloated; and weedy Goebbels. The bands drowned any lack of cheering, but there wasn't one around me, for either Ribbentrop or Goebbels, though Goering got more than his chief. The crowd yelled: 'Hermann!' with the same sincerity as we cheer the King.

When it was over I joined Ronnie Panton, the *Daily Express* Berlin correspondent. Here was an example of the British hospitality that I'd seen so much of. He'd never met me before that day I arrived in Berlin, but not only did he volunteer any information about Germany, but also he took me to his home for dinner and afterwards showed me the night spots. He believed war was inevitable. He said that the Wilhelmstrasse was quite incapable of believing that we were ready to fight them. Hitler had in any case gone so far in his Polish demands that he could not now draw back.

'There is no sign of political upheaval here,' he said, 'and so long as the going is good Hitler will stay. But all of us correspondents are convinced of one thing. If there is a war, and Germany gets a major defeat, the present regime won't last three months after it. Wishful thinking, however, that the country will disintegrate by itself is sheer nonsense.'

Panton was in Copenhagen when the Germans marched into Denmark. He had no chance of escaping. It can be only hoped that

283

the Nazis won't try to revenge themselves on him for the stories he has written condemning their regime.

I went on from Berlin to Cologne, where I had spent five years of my childhood during the time my father was serving in the Army of Occupation. Shortly before we got into the station a man in my compartment started a conversation with me by asking: 'Are you a Swede?' (Oddly enough, an SS man in Cologne, of whom more later, asked me the same question.) On learning I was English he began the usual talk of: 'We don't want war'; and he pointed to a scar on his face, saying: 'I got this when one of your submarines torpedoed my ship ... but I don't bear you any grudge because of it.' He asked me what I was going to do and what I was going to see during my few hours in the town. I told him I was going to visit my old home at Bayenthal Gürtel on the Üfer, and also the Opera House where we used to hear the great singers of Germany night after night. We said goodbye at the station and I thought no more about him. I took a tram down the Rhine front to the Bismarck statue and surveyed the vacant plot of ground where once stood our house, and then returned to the Dom Platz with the intention of finding my way to the Opera House. My memory was bad, and I stopped a man to ask for directions. It was as I was speaking to him that the SS man came up. He said that as he himself was going that way he would escort me. For half an hour I walked beside him through the streets, discoursing in German about current events. He, too, said no thinking German wanted war. 'We have so much to do inside our country,' he said, 'that we cannot worry about taking other countries.' He was polite and most friendly towards me; but when we reached the Opera House he gave me a surprise. He smartly clicked his heels and bowed stiffly. Then he said in the most perfect English: 'It's been a great pleasure to be of help to you. Goodbye!' I gaped at him. 'Hell,' I said, 'why have you been letting me struggle with my German?' He looked at me, almost fiercely. 'In Germany,' he said curtly, 'we speak only German.'

I watched him for a second as he crossed the Sachsen Ring before I turned into the Opera House. I had taken about a dozen steps when suddenly from behind a pillar appeared the man of the train. He took off his hat and smiled at me with such an air of surprise that for a second I thought it might have been just a strange coincidence that he was there. 'This is a pleasure,' he said in German. 'We must celebrate our meeting. Come with me to the café.' He took me upstairs and over a glass of lager he oozed propaganda. Again I heard about this wish for no war; and about the trust of the people that the Führer wouldn't lead them into it. And, cunningly, he told me that the people derided Goebbels, and that Goering was just a nice hail-fellow-well-met sort of man; and that Ribbentrop was hated. He was lyrical in his praise of what Hitler had done for the people ... the slums cleared away, holidays with pay for all, opera seats at prices low enough for the poorest working man, etc., and he ended with the words: 'Can you possibly believe that a man who has done all that would now lead his country to destruction? Because war would mean destruction whether we conquered or lost.'

He would not let me pay for the drinks, nor would he let me pay for the taxi in which he afterwards took me to the station. 'I want in my own small way,' he said, 'to show friendliness to your country.' It was a good thing that he did. For I had run out of money. My funds had at last come to an end; and I had had to wire home for £5 to be sent to Paris so as to pay for my ticket to London.

6

Not only £5 was waiting for me when I reached Paris. My mother was there too. I came into the hotel in the Rue du Colisée which I had given as my address, and there she was, sitting in the lounge. That sudden sight of her will remain vividly in my memory all my life. I'd been a long time among strangers, among people whose companionship, because of its brevity, could never be much more than frivolous and superficial. And if on occasions I'd met someone who shared my outlook, and who laughed at the same things, no sooner had we become friends than it was time to move on; on to a new city where I had to start all over again. Such was the penalty of travel.

So when I saw my mother I felt how a dumb man would feel if he were suddenly able to speak. I was able to unload the multitude of thoughts and experiences that only someone who knew me intimately could possibly be interested in; and for three hours I lived again my journey across the world. Then afterwards, when we'd had dinner, we strolled out into the warm June evening down the Champs-Élysées across the Place de la Concorde to the Avenue beside the Seine.

I remember her asking me how I thought I'd benefited from my year away and my reply that it would take months and months before I'd know how much I'd got from it. 'At the moment,' I said, 'I cannot see it in perspective. It's like looking at a large painting a yard from the canvas. Or like being a man who has just read the Bible for the first time from the beginning to the end. He is confused by its riches, and it will only be after study and contemplation that he will separate the truths, so that they become clear in his mind. In the same sort of way I hope to discover what this journey has done for me.'

Then, I remember, she asked me what I was

going to do next. And I didn't answer at once. On that day I'd set out for New York my mood had been a holiday one; and the weeks that followed in America had been lighthearted, and the things I had done could hardly be described as being very serious. And then, too, in the South Seas I was only a casual adventurer with no cares on my shoulders, and with a sense of irresponsibility that kept me unaware that the force of history might interrupt the independence of my life. True, I was conscious of the wounds of the world, but I didn't believe they would ever affect me personally; just as a racing-car driver believes that accidents will happen to others but never to him. I imagined that in the immediate years to follow I would be able to go on fulfilling my way of life. I did not imagine that my independence would be cut into pieces by the ravages of war.

But gradually, as my journey led me from New Zealand to Australia, from China to Japan, from Manchukuo to Germany, there grew a heaviness of heart within me. From looking objectively on the scarred scene of the nations' quarrels, I awoke to being aware that my life was a unit in the quarrel, that I would have to face the hell that was coming with the same realism as a small boy faces a beating. And as I stood there with my mother, beside the gentle, idle peace of the river and the dark shadows of the old bridges that stretched across the water to Montparnasse, I saw in my mind the strutting, threatening figures of Berlin, the myriads of uniforms, the planes roaring low over the roofs; and I knew there was no escape. Like millions of others I was caught in a trap; but unlike millions of others I felt I was able to say, no matter what future there lay before me, that I had lived.

But I answered my mother's question by saying it was too soon to know what I would do next, there being no object in burdening her with my gloomy thoughts; and then, taking her by the arm, I said: 'There's at any rate one thing I can tell you. I've come home a bit of a jingoist. I know now that Britain with all her faults is the best of the lot. And tomorrow, when I see the cliffs of Dover, I'll have the proverbial tears in my eyes.'

And by heavens it was so! When next day, on the far horizon, I saw the thin white line of cliffs, I had a lump in my throat. And just as when I'd left I'd had a brandy to stop me making a fool of myself, so had I then.